THE NEW TEACHER INDUCTION BOOK

How to Recruit, Train, and Retain New Teachers

Harry K. Wong and Rosemary T. Wong

HARRY K. WONG PUBLICATIONS, INC.
www.EffectiveTeaching.com

This book is printed on environmentally friendly paper. Join us in making a choice to save the planet.

Copyright © 2024 Harry K. Wong Publications, Inc.

All rights reserved. No part of this publication or any related materials referenced herein may be stored in a retrieval system, transmitted, reproduced in any form or by any means, electronic, mechanical, photocopying, recording, or otherwise, or be the basis for any derivative works, without the prior agreement and written permission of the publisher.

ISBN: 978-1-7346490-1-7

Library of Congress Control Number: 2023949104

10 9 8 7 6 5 4 3 2 1

Printed in Canada by Friesens

Executive Producer: Rosemary T. Wong
Graphic Design: Mark Van Slyke
Editor: Katharine Sturak
Administrative Assistant: Lacey Imes

HARRY K. WONG PUBLICATIONS, INC.
943 North Shoreline Boulevard
Mountain View, CA 94043-1932
T: 650-965-7896 F: 650-965-7890
www.HarryWong.com

Dedication

J. Robert "Bob" Hendricks

Meeting you was one of the defining moments in our lives that continues to bring value to our work. The Flowing Wells Institute for Teacher Renewal and Growth that you shared with us forty years ago was that "aha" moment that was so obvious, but sadly to this day, is still an afterthought. Your dedication to elevating the profession is inspiring. Your friendship through the years is treasured.

Bob's reach has gone far beyond the Flowing Wells Unified School District. Such a difference maker.
https://coe.arizona.edu/person/j-robert-hendricks

Contents

Retaining New Teachers

1. You Win with Teachers 3
2. What Is New Teacher Induction? 12
3. Mentoring Is Not Induction 25

Induction Programs That Retain and Develop

4. A School with No Attrition 37
5. Moberly School District 41
6. Flowing Wells Unified School District 45
7. The Stay Interview 52

High-Performing Induction Programs

8. High-Performing School Systems 59
9. High-Performing Companies 72
10. Return on Investment 77

Developing New Teachers

11. First Five Minutes of the First Day 87
12. Induction Program Essentials 97
13. Recruiting New Teachers 108
14. How to Start and Sustain an Induction Program 114

Afterword 122

Research tells us . . .

That when teachers receive well-designed professional development, an average of forty-nine hours spread over six to twelve months, they increase student achievement by a much as twenty-one percentile points.

Workshops that are considered as "one-shot," "drive-by," or obligatory meetings lasting fourteen hours or less show no statistically significant effect on student learning.

The most effective professional-development programs are job-embedded and provide teachers with collaborative learning, active learning, and sustained learning.[1]

> *Like so many districts, many have relaxed their teacher certificate requirements. They now have long-term subs, bus drivers, and teacher's assistants serving as full-time teachers. And this is all done without providing any training or attention to classroom management or professional development.*
>
> A new teacher

Welcome teachers into the profession and train them with a **New Teacher Induction Program** that will produce truly effective teachers. Every student in your school, in your school district deserves nothing less.

---

[1] Vanessa Vega, "Teacher Development Research Review: Keys to Educator Success," *Edutopia*, November 1, 2015, https://www.edutopia.org/teacher-development-research-keys-success.

Retaining New Teachers

1 **You Win with Teachers**
Trained, effective teachers are a school's greatest asset. 3

2 **What Is New Teacher Induction?**
The role of an induction program is to train, support, and retain effective teachers. 12

3 **Mentoring Is Not Induction**
Mentoring is haphazard and individual; induction is collaborative and collegial. 25

1 You Win with Teachers

Trained, effective teachers are a school's greatest asset.

The Moberly New Teacher Induction Program

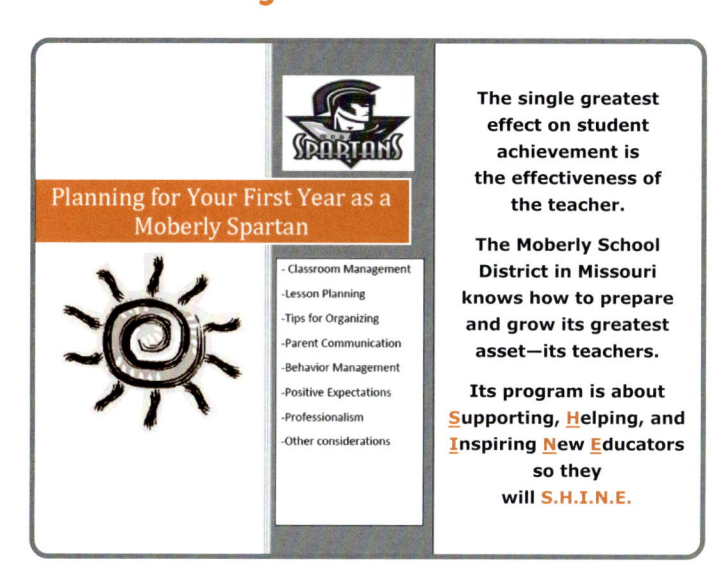

> The single greatest effect on student achievement is the effectiveness of the teacher.
>
> The Moberly School District in Missouri knows how to prepare and grow its greatest asset—its teachers.
>
> Its program is about **S**upporting, **H**elping, and **I**nspiring **N**ew **E**ducators so they will S.H.I.N.E.

The Moberly School District is a small, rural district in Missouri. It has had a new teacher induction program for well over ten years. The program, **S.H.I.N.E., Supporting, Helping, and Improving New Educators**, is monitored by a teacher, **Tara Link**. The program provides new teacher support through tutoring and coaching in the curriculum and culture of the Moberly School District.

The most telling comments come from first- and second-year teachers who talk to their college friends and learn the support they are receiving exceeds that of their counterparts in other districts.

The Moberly retention rate for beginning teachers is above 83 percent, which exceeds the state average of 60 percent over the past ten years.

I Left at the End of the School Year

I was hired by the district human resources office and assigned to a school. There was no preschool meeting for the newly hired teachers. I showed up on the first day for teachers with all the other teachers on the staff.

There were over three hundred teachers in the auditorium for the first-day meeting at which the superintendent welcomed all the new teachers and asked us to stand.

We received the obligatory round of applause. Then we sat. After the meeting, I walked slowly to my classroom.

There was no induction program, and I did not see my principal until two weeks after school began as we passed in the hall. He did not provide any kind of a guide as to how the school functions or who taught at the school.

I never saw another teacher's classroom. I survived in isolation. I had no idea if what I was doing was right or wrong. I left at the end of the school year.

— A new teacher

One of the problems in education is more than finding enough teachers. It's keeping them.

To retain teachers, schools must implement new teacher induction programs to develop the capacity of teachers to become highly effective teachers. **Effective teachers tend to stay.**

New teacher induction programs support new teachers and impart the fundamentals of effective teaching.

The hallmark of an effective school or district is that they have an extensive and sustained professional training program for its teachers, its human capital.

Defining New Teacher Induction

New Teacher Induction is simply the common-sense method used to help newly hired teachers fit into the school or district culture (if one exists, and it should) and curriculum (if one exists, and it should) and succeed as a teacher.

What Do You Want Me to Teach?

What am I supposed to teach?

Beth was so excited. Her family had moved into a new community. Her husband had a new job; the children were enrolled in their respective schools; and Beth got a job at the district's middle school.

She showed up at the school's office and was greeted by the school secretary who gave her the schedule and keys to her classroom. Beth asked, "Can I have a copy of the school's curriculum?"

The secretary replied, "Humma, humma ... Oh, you'll figure it out."

No one in the school ever helped Beth "figure it out." She left at the end of the school year.

She Teaches Them What to Teach

Provide new teachers with a roadmap for success.

Amanda Bivens was appointed as a Grade 3–5 Instructional Coach in the Dyer County School District in Tennessee after teaching for ten years. In her first year, she coached five teachers, all of whom were rehired. Since then, she has coached fifty-four teachers, and all have been rehired. The district also has a K–2 coach, middle school coach, high school coach, and literacy coach. They all work together almost daily.

The investment the district made in hiring the coaches has more than repaid itself in that there has been no attrition of their new teachers. Not only that, they have all become effective teachers.

This methodology occurs when employees are hired at McDonald's, United Airlines, or a small convenience store. The first question asked of those newly hired is, "What do you want me to do?" They expect to be trained and they are.

The Significance of the Teacher

The single greatest effect on student achievement is the teacher to whom a student gets assigned.[1]

Teacher effectiveness is the single largest factor affecting the academic growth of students. Yet in too many schools and school districts, we put teachers in a classroom and hope by dumb luck that they become effective teachers. They are given no direction, possibly no curriculum, and whatever is shared has been cobbled together by the principal.

According to the **MetLife Survey of the American Teacher** (2009), teachers in the United States work alone. On average they spend 93 percent of their time in school working in isolation. Their day-to-day work is disconnected from the efforts of their colleagues, and their mediocre professional development prevents any substantial education improvement taking place with regard to their students' learning needs.

When new teachers fail, the school and the district fail. Over two hundred studies support the position that teacher quality is the most critical factor by which to improve student achievement. A **UCLA** study attributed to

The teacher is the difference in student success.

There is no collaboration or connection when working in isolation.

John Goodlad reviewed forty years of educational innovations and did not find a single one that contributed significantly to student achievement. **The only factor that raised student achievement was the effectiveness of a teacher.**

Induction and Learning Are Immediate

When a newly hired teacher shows up for the first day of school in Japan or Finland, the teacher is escorted to a large room where all the teachers have their desks and share a common office surrounded by experienced teachers they can consult to design a lesson.

They do not have to create their own lessons as the lessons are collaborative endeavors. Groups of teachers create and even collaboratively teach the lesson. In Japan this is called "Lesson Study."

In Finland, the teachers are "didacticians," (the science of teaching and instruction), people who can connect teaching effectiveness with sound evidence. New teachers immediately learn how to work in problem-solving groups that are involved in a continuous cycle of planning, action, reflection, and evaluation. Collaboration is structured into the school day as Finnish teachers usually meet weekly to plan and develop curriculum. Induction and learning are immediate and ongoing and has been in effect for decades.

No one teaches in isolation in Finland, Japan, and other high-performing countries. **The culture in Finland and Japan is that you are part of a welcoming professional network, sharing ideas and best practices.**

In many other countries, all teachers share a common office.

> *The most valuable resource teachers have is each other. Without collaboration our growth is limited to our own perspectives.*
>
> **Robert John Meehan**

The Perils of Isolation

There is some good news for new teachers at most schools in the United States. They are considered an equal with all the other teachers on their very first day of their teaching careers. There is no formal hierarchy.

However, here is the frightening news.

- Beginning teachers are expected to assume the same tasks and responsibilities as the most seasoned teacher on the staff.
- Beginning teachers are expected to perform the full complement of duties—immediately.
- Beginning teachers are expected to be fully prepared to teach on the first day of school and then improve each year.
- Beginning teachers are expected to be experienced, veteran teachers without administrative supervision or training.

New Teacher Humiliation

Teachers in the United States are typically hired because there is a slot to fill, not because the school has an explicit mission to fulfill. Sadly, once they are hired, many new teachers are forgotten and left to fend for themselves. The teacher is given the key to a room and told to enter and teach or, in the case of many new teachers, enter and survive.

The unspoken message to new teachers is figure it out yourself, do it yourself, and keep it to yourself!

> *I received one day of orientation, during which I mostly filled out forms. No one officially welcomed me or the other three new teachers to my school. In fact, the veteran teachers received us with skepticism, at best. Apparently, I was assigned a mentor, but she was busy with her own classroom.*
>
> **Christina Asquith**
> (taught for one year)

Sadly, once they are hired, many new teachers are forgotten and left to fend for themselves 93 percent of the their time.

> ### New Teacher Humiliation
>
> The first year of teaching is the most critical. New teachers feel isolated, vulnerable, deeply concerned with how they will be perceived, and thus afraid to ask for help.
>
> When they are hired, they are given a key, told which room is theirs, and are given no support.
>
> They are given the worst assignments.
> They feel frightened.
> They feel humiliated.
> They are given no assistance and mentoring is not assistance.
> They want someone to give them hope and tell them when their hardships will end.

Beginning teachers rarely make easy or smooth transitions into teaching. Often they are hired at the last moment, left isolated in their classrooms, and given little help, resulting in attrition rates among new teachers that are five times higher than among experienced teachers.

It is a lamentable fact of life in our public schools that new teachers are assigned the more difficult classes and the more difficult students and put in the worst classrooms. Beginning teachers must work with the toughest clients and take on the most troublesome non-teaching duties.

Even worse, there is a shortage of meaningful support on behalf of new teachers.

New teachers who are "left to their own devices" feel alone, confused, and inadequate. They often avoid asking for help, fearing the negative perceptions of other teachers. **Thus, many leave teaching and the dream they had of making a difference in the lives of children—because no one made a difference in their life.**

The Futility of Fads

Instead of developing effective teachers with a foundational skill set focused on implementing a coherent curriculum, billions of dollars have been spent over the past seventy-five years chasing silver bullets that are shot at incoherent, random reform targets hoping to save American education. Teachers are forced to devote their time implementing the latest miracle cure, fad, innovation, or technology that has been forced on the school.

Teachers come to school to teach, and students come to school to learn. Instead of having induction programs that teach teachers how to instruct effectively, we have a system that is obsessed with searching for reforms or the next technology that will do the teaching for the teacher.

I want to do what is right, but no one ever taught me how to do things.

Absolutely no educational system in the world, except in the United States, is run on the endless, repetitive, futile cycle of chasing one fad after another, after another, after another . . . .

Do you remember these reforms, each with its fifteen minutes of notoriety—flipped classroom, self-esteem, whole language, personalized learning, and hemisphericity? When are we going to teach the curriculum?

The Necessity of Induction Programs

Fads and innovations do not teach students; teachers teach students.

Most teachers go through four phases during their professional career.

1. **Fantasy** when the teacher has illusions of improbable success
2. **Survival** when the teacher is trying to cope in the classroom
3. **Mastery** when instruction has been mastered by the teacher
4. **Impact** when the teacher is making a significant difference in students' lives

The purpose of a new teacher induction program is to guide new teachers out of Survival towards Mastery and beyond.

If new teachers fail, it is the school and school district that has failed because no organized effort has been made to develop the capabilities and performance of teachers.

> It is a source of continuing amazement to me that almost all the discourse regarding restructuring and reforming schools over the last decade has emphasized every conceivable form of change and virtually ignored the obvious: getting better teachers. It's the teacher, stupid![2]
>
> Martin Haberman
> University of Wisconsin, Milwaukee

They Just Gave Me the Keys

> I am a friendly person and I like to talk with people, but when I'm here at school I feel I'm all alone. When I started here, I did not see the principal. As I arrived at the office, I asked for someone to speak to and explained that I was a new teacher.
>
> This person just pointed to a certain direction where I met the principal's secretary. I told her I was a new teacher, and she gave me the keys and told me to go to a certain building.
>
> No one welcomed me. No one escorted me; I had to find it myself. When I found my classroom, I soon learned that I would be in it alone for the school year.
>
> When I was hired, I was not told what to teach and that I was supposed to create my own Syllabus and Lesson Plans. When I asked for help, they just told me, "You'll learn."
>
> I turned in my keys after teaching for one year.
>
> Janis Wagner

Janis could have been saved if her district had offered an induction program.

This is a long list of some of the innovations that have been tried throughout the years—and are still being tried with little or no improvement in the quality of teaching and learning. They have all been created by caring and well-meaning people, but few have made a dent in improving student learning. When another one makes an appearance, the development of teachers and students grinds to a halt to allow for the implementation of the new fad or opinionated agenda. Well-intentioned teachers become at-risk teachers because they are thrown into an unfamiliar, confusing situation. They have to scramble to keep up with all the everyday expectations, plus incorporate a new program, to just survive.

21st Century curriculum
4-day school week
Academy-based learning
Accomplished-based learning
Achievement-based assessment
Adaptive assessment
Adaptive learning
Adaptive technology
After-school programs
Alignment of assessment
Alternative assessment
Argument Driven Inquiry
Art-centered learning
Assertive discipline
Assessment-based achievement
Audio Lingual Method
Blended learning
Block scheduling
Brain compatibility
Care-based practices
Case-based learning
Challenge-based learning
Clerestory Learning
Community-based learning
Computer-based reading
Concerns-based improvement
Constructivism
Culturally responsive teaching
Curriculum-based measurements
Customized instruction
Data driven instruction
Deficit/Abundance Model
Design-based learning
Detracking
Differentiated instruction
Digital-based learning
Discovery method
Diversity-based curriculum
Dual-enrollment program
Earth-bound education
Embodied learning
Emotional intelligence
Evidence-based education
Experiential education
Flipped classroom
Four-day schools
Game-based learning
Games-based curriculum
Garden-based learning
Goals 2000
Hemisphericity
High-leveraged content
High-stakes testing
Hybrid learning
Inquiry-based learning
Interdisciplinary teaching
Land-based learning
Learning ecosystems
Learning to learn
Linked learning
Longer school day/year
Looping
Magnet schools
Maker movement
Mass customized learning
Microschools
Modular scheduling
Multiage classrooms
Multi-classroom teachers
Multicultural education
Multidimensional assessment
Multiple intelligence
Nature-based learning
Needs-based education
Open classroom
Opensource learning
Outcomes-based education
Paradigm shift
Passion-based learning
PBIS
Performance assessment
Personal learning environment
Personalized blended learning
Personalized instruction
Picting
Play-based learning
Portfolio assessment
Practice-focused curriculum
Principle-based education
Problem-based learning
Proficiency-based learning
Project-based learning
Reality therapy
Reciprocal accountability
Reggio Emilia Approach
Relationship-centered approach
Renaissance science
Restorative justice
Revolutionary learning
School choice
Self-directed learning
Self-esteem
Self-regulated education
Service-based learning
Shared decision making
Single-gender classes
Small class/school size
Social-emotional learning
Start school day later
Strength-based learning
Student-led learning
Studio-based learning
Systems thinking skills
Teaching for social justice
Team-based learning
Technology-based learning
Thematic-integrated instruction
Theme-based learning
Three-dimensional teaching
Total Quality Management (TQM)
Virtual learning
Whole language
Work-based learning
Year-round schools
Zero tolerance
Zombie-based learning

We Keep Riding Dead Horses

Common sense tells you that when you discover you are riding a dead horse the best strategy is to dismount.

Education systems, however, continue to carry on with dead horses in the following ways. Why? Because that's the way it's always been done!

- Give the horse a new name such as "blended horses."
- Throw out the sage-on-the-stage and give the horse a mentor.
- Change riders.
- Say things like, "Riding a horse comes naturally."
- Appoint a committee to study the "whole horse."
- Arrange to visit other schools to see how they ride dead horses.
- Increase the common core standards to include riding dead horses.
- Create an "action research team" to revive the dead horse.
- Create in-service training sessions to increase riding ability.
- Change the mission statement to declare, "This horse is not dead."
- Bring in an outside consultant to ride the dead horse.
- Install new technology to improve dead horse speed.
- Apply for a grant to reduce class size for all horses.
- Apply for more counselors, social workers, and aides for the horses.
- Tell the dead horse to design its own course and gallop at its own pace.

There is nothing within a school that has more impact on children, in terms of skills development, self-confidence, and classroom behavior, than the personal and professional growth of teachers.

You Win with Teachers

Teachers represent the greatest asset of a school. Ask any administrator to name the greatest asset of their school and most often you will get answers like money or a program. Rarely will you hear that a school's greatest assets are its teachers. Research proves this point repeatedly—**teacher instructional effectiveness is the most critical component of improving student achievement and closing the achievement gap**. For student learning to be effective, a school district must invest in its greatest asset—effective teachers.

Famed business guru **Peter Drucker**, who coined the term "human capital," considered people assets. Human capital is not measured by accumulated physical assets, but by knowledge, skills, and attitudes. Business leaders know that the better their people—their assets—the more successful the company. Human capital is the wealth and future of a company. People are its major assets—just as teachers are a school's greatest assets.

Teacher effectiveness is the predominant factor affecting school quality.[3]

Hall of Fame football coach **Joe Gibbs** puts it short and sweet, "You win with people." Translated for schools, "You win with teachers." You don't win with programs, technology, or structural changes. The only meaningful factor that increases student achievement is an effective teacher.

10 • THE New Teacher Induction Book

To produce effective teachers, schools must implement an induction process designed to train and acculturate new teachers—and those teachers new to the school—to the core business of your school—its academic standards, vision, and culture.

> **If you want students to learn, you win with teachers.**

You win with teachers.

Endnotes

[1] Steven G. Rivkin, Eric A. Hanushek, and John F. Kain, "Teachers, Schools, and Academic Achievement," *Econometrica* 73, no. 2 (March 2005): 417–458.

[2] Martin Haberman, "Preparing Teachers for the Real World of Urban Schools," *The Educational Forum* 58, no. 2 (Winter 1994).

[3] Eric A. Hanushek, Paul E. Peterson, Laura M. Talpey, and Ludger Woessmann, "The Achievement Gap Fails to Close," *Education Next* 19, no. 3 (Summer 2019).

2 What Is New Teacher Induction?

The role of an induction program is to train, support, and retain effective teachers.

EducationWeek
RECRUITMENT & RETENTION

How Bad Is the Teacher Shortage? What Two New Studies Say

Tens of thousands of students are being taught by uncertified teachers.[1]

New Teacher Induction Is Professional Development

The first phase of professional development for a new teacher is induction, a process that typically runs two to three years and then flows seamlessly into a life-long professional development program. **Effective induction programs ensure that new teachers are teaching effectively from the very first day of school.**

> "I attended this national principal's meeting and there were barely six people in the session on new teachers. Conversely, the session on teacher burnout and how to get rid of them was filled.
>
> I'm a quiet person, but after listening to the group complain about *these* teachers, I said to the group, "If you had provided a new teacher induction program twenty-five years ago, you wouldn't have this problem today."
>
> Jeanette Darby
> Birmingham, Alabama

Start new teacher induction before students arrive to keep teachers in the profession.

An induction program is a comprehensive, multiyear process designed to train and acculturate new teachers, or any teachers new to the school or district, to the academic standards and vision of the school district.

School districts with a low teacher attrition rate have an organized, multiyear, sustained program to train, support, collaboratively engage, and retain new recruits.

Induction includes introducing new teachers to their responsibilities and the missions and philosophies of their district and school. The training helps new teachers get up to speed as easily and quickly as possible, ease their anxieties, and maximize their effectiveness.

Learning to be an effective teacher requires time, effort, resources, support, and every staff person's commitment to fostering an environment where everyone is treated with respect, valued for their input, set up for success, and able to grow and thrive in their chosen careers.

> **Teachers stay with a school where they feel part of a collaborative mission to succeed.**

A successful induction program produces these results.

- It reduces the difficulty of the transition into teaching.
- It provides instruction in effective classroom management and instructional techniques.
- It promotes the district's culture—its philosophies, missions, policies, procedures, and goals.
- It maximizes the retention rate of highly qualified teachers.

The Benefits of Belonging

Humans are social creatures. Most have a deep desire to connect with others—family, friends, and coworkers. Belonging is a basic human need.

New teachers want to be part of a team and part of a culture. They want to belong. To create this sense,

Belonging feels as good as a warm coat on a winter's day.

this feeling, create a structured, sustained, intensive professional development program that allows new teachers to observe others, to be observed by others, and to be part of networks or study groups where all teachers share together, grow together, and learn to respect each other's work.

We can learn from the practices of high-performing countries. (See Chapter 8.) These systems involve teachers in the learning process. Planning for student growth and achievement is a collaborative endeavor with regularly scheduled meetings. Designing lessons and developing curriculum are part of a teacher's workday. It is not done in isolation in the wee hours of the morning.

> **In high-performing countries, teachers meet regularly to share ideas and best practices.**

Training programs are the norm for most jobs. Businesses train their new workers from the day they join until the day they leave. Ask the fire chief, the store manager, or hospital executive what they do with new employees. Ask the baseball manager, construction foreman, or senior partner in a law firm what they do. Ask the leaders at corporations and in the retail and hospitality sectors. They all will tell you that every employee is trained and the training continues until the employee leaves the business.

Education should be no different. The purpose of the induction process is to immerse new teachers in the district's culture and to unite them with everyone in the district as a cohesive, supportive instructional team. New teachers quickly become a part of the district's "family."

It Starts Before Induction

First-year teachers can be as effective as typical third-year teachers if those new teachers spend their student teaching experience in the classroom of a highly effective teacher.[2]

A preservice teacher paired with a highly effective teacher will be exposed to the components of a well-structured classroom and an academic environment where students thrive. They'll carry that expectation of success to their first teaching position and expect to be supported to achieve their dream.

A new teacher induction program is the keeper of dreams.

Collaborative Impact

There is overwhelming research on the instructional methods that enhance student learning. This research has been done by thousands of education professionals worldwide. **John Hattie** has done the monumental task of compiling and correlating all this research in *Visible Learning—A Synthesis of Over 800 Meta-Analyses Relating to Achievement.*

According to his list of influences that affect student achievement, the second highest influence on student achievement is collective efficacy. **In this book it will be referred to as collaborative impact. Collaborative impact has an effect-size of 1.57.**[3] It refers to the power of teachers working together, designing, implementing, and assessing lessons, to continuously explore ways to be more effective in the classroom.

Influences with Positive Effects on Student Achievement[4]

Influence	Effect Size
Teacher estimation	1.62
Collaborative impact	**1.57**
Self-reported grades	1.33
Teacher clarity	0.75
Reciprocal teaching	0.74
Feedback	0.70
Direct instruction	0.60
Spaced vs. massed practice	0.60
Mastery learning	0.57

When teachers work together they produce one of the highest impacts on student learning and achievement.[5]

Collaborative impact is defined as the "judgment of teachers that they can organize and execute the course of action required to have a positive effect on students."[6]

Collaborative impact is more than
- three times as powerful and predictive of student learning and achievement than socioeconomic status,
- double the effect of prior achievement, and
- triple the effect of home environment and parental involvement.

Collaborative impact is very powerful because it guides educators' actions. Some teachers believe that their school would be successful if it had smaller class sizes, more counselors and social workers, or more technology. This is a survival attitude and very little will be accomplished to influence student achievement. However, if a school staff shares a sense of collaborative impact, that is research based for proven success, then they have a greater likelihood of positively impacting student learning, regardless of other internal or external influences.

> The most powerful influence on student achievement occurs when teachers work together and purposefully focus on instruction that will make an impact.

Education Is a Collaborative Endeavor

To experience professional success in life, shift your mindset away from independence toward collaboration. Wisdom is gleaned from others.

> Collaboration is the key to lifelong success.

In the United States, teachers are typically viewed as independent operators, expected to do a good job behind closed doors. Worse yet, new teachers seldom see another classroom. "I never sat in anyone else's classroom even once," laments a first-year teacher. "Mine is the only teaching style I know. I felt that sometimes I was reinventing the wheel." Loneliness and lack of support exacerbate the problems of beginning teachers.

With the constant talk of differentiation, personalization, and individualization, we take dedicated, caring teachers—especially new teachers—give them no or minimal induction, and isolate them in a classroom, never to interact with even the teacher next door. They are expected to do a good job behind closed doors. There is no culture of belonging. Collaboration is rare.

Collaboration closes the effective teacher gap, leads to increased teacher satisfaction, greater student success, and elevates the profession.

Yet collaboration is the most effective way for teachers to make progress professionally and achieve results in their classrooms.

- A school's collaborative culture is the key to success. Schools in all high-ranking countries foster teamwork and cooperation.
- When teachers work together, they are capable of producing extraordinary results in student learning and achievement.
- The most powerful influence on student achievement occurs when teachers

Chapter 2: What Is New Teacher Induction?

They Had Never Seen Katie Teach

"Three teachers had been teaching next door to each other for seven to nine years—Katie in the middle, and the other two on either side of her—yet not once had the two teachers ever been in Katie's classroom while she was teaching. The structure of the school was such that they were being excluded from the knowledge that Katie could have shared and that might have helped make them all better teachers.

Katie was an exceptional fourth-grade teacher. Honestly, she was the single best classroom teacher I've ever witnessed. As she taught, she seemed to be tapping into multiple brains simultaneously, quickly analyzing what different students needed and responding in the moment to meet those needs. Add to that her warmth and humor, and her classroom was alive with learning.

I visited her classroom more than twenty years ago after multiple people recommended her to me. Her principal was effusive in his praise for her work and, as I arrived, he said one of his hardest jobs every fall was explaining to dozens of parents why their children would not be in Katie's classroom that year.

As I was leaving Katie's classroom, the other two fourth-grade teachers were in the hallway and summoned me over. At first, I thought they just wanted to say goodbye. We chatted briefly, then one of them asked me, kind of shyly, "What makes Katie such a great teacher?"

I was a little taken aback by that question. Were they trying to figure out if I knew what I was doing? That wasn't it at all. After a few more moments, I realized that they had no idea why their colleague was so often recognized for her excellence. They had never seen Katie teach. I was dumbstruck.

This trio had been colleagues for years. One teacher had worked in the classroom next to Katie's for seven years; the other teacher had worked on the other side of Katie for nine years and in two different schools. Not once had either of them ever been in Katie's classroom while she was teaching.

That encounter was really pivotal for me, one of those experiences that has come to shape so much of what I believe about teachers and teaching. At the core is my belief that teachers learn a great deal about how to work better as they work every day. They deepen their knowledge about students and teaching every time they step in front of a classroom. Although practitioners can learn a great deal from researchers of all stripes, practitioners also can learn a great deal from each other, especially when they have the opportunities and structures to do so.

As I drove away from Katie's school, I thought about how demoralized her colleagues must have felt about being excluded from the knowledge that Katie could have shared and that might have helped make them better teachers. So near, and yet so far.

I thought about the students in that school. Although it was wonderful that Katie's students had the opportunity to learn from such an extraordinary teacher, her presence in that building did not help the dozens of other fourth graders in that school. Those children didn't benefit at all from having this exemplary teacher in their school because her knowledge and her skills were never shared with her teaching colleagues. Didn't those children also have the right to benefit from what was known by an exemplary teacher?

What of the several hundred other fourth graders in the other six or seven elementary schools in that district? Shouldn't they also have been able to benefit from Katie's knowledge and skills?

Years after visiting Katie's classroom, I stumbled across a comment by Roland Barth, who said: "I wonder how many children's lives might be saved if we educators disclosed what we know to each other."

Keeping an exemplary teacher's knowledge isolated inside a classroom isn't just poor practice, it's almost malpractice. If you want to be an agent for change in your school or your district, work now to ensure that no teacher works in such isolation. Be an advocate for sharing what you know. Ask to observe another teacher teach because of what you will learn. Invite others to observe you and offer you feedback on how you can improve. Write articles and make presentations about what you're learning from your work.

By opening the doors to their practice, teachers demonstrate the value they place on their own learning and their belief that they have much to share with others.[7]

Joan Richardson
Former Editor, *KAPPAN*

purposefully focus on developing effective instruction based upon using proven techniques and strategies.
- Building the group's collective impact to achieve schoolwide goals must be the highest priority for teachers and administrators.
- It is incumbent that schools create a culture where collaborative impact is focused on pursuing a common vision for student learning.
- Effective schools develop and sustain a collaborative culture where staff know what they want to accomplish and speak a common language to achieve their aims.

In addition, in schools where collaborative impact is present, students are less likely to be suspended or be removed from classrooms as a result of misbehavior.[8] Where there is a shared sense of collaborative impact, student achievement improves because teachers
- have more positive attitudes toward professional development,
- exhibit deeper implementation of evidence-based instructional strategies, and
- have a stronger focus and commitment to academic achievement.

When new teachers visit a demonstration classroom, they see firsthand what organization is needed for an effective school year.

Chapter 2: What Is New Teacher Induction? • 17

To improve learning outcomes, we must focus on making schools better. The only sure way to do that is with an induction program that encourages and supports teachers to be their very best.[9]

The Power of Teamwork

Every successful sports team will tell you that every player is an individual with their own talents and foibles, but when they are out in the field, they play together as a team. Teamwork is fostered during induction when people work together for the greater good, meaning that each person is willing to forgo their own ego, their own agenda, and make decisions that are truly in the best interests of students. **Phil Jackson**, one of the great coaches in NBA history said, "The strength of the team is each individual member. The strength of each member is the team."

Teamwork is what separates effective schools from ineffective schools.

Teachers remain when they feel supported by administrators, have strong bonds of connection to colleagues, and are aggressively pursuing a collective vision or set of practices and values that are committed to student learning. The era of isolated teaching is over.

It is not possible to create and sustain a professional learning community when there is a revolving door of new teachers and administrators joining a faculty every year. High turnover will diminish the sense of continuity and coherence that is the hallmark of effective schools.

Ineffective schools have no culture, or rather, they have a culture that produces no results because its practices and values revolve around the survival of individual administrators and teachers.

Just think how much money would be saved and how much more effective our teachers and schools would be if new teachers experienced an induction process of collaborators who learned and improved together.

An induction process that fosters collaboration and teacher networks, and provides professional development and study groups, achieves far greater results in teacher learning than individual mentors. Induction brings new teachers up to speed as fast as possible and maximizes their effectiveness. Effective schools know that when they train and support their teachers, the teachers will stay where they feel successful and respected.

Improved student learning occurs when schools harness the collective intelligence, creativity, and genius of their teachers in collaborative teams.

When teachers meet in teams and are laser-focused on student results, they ultimately create an impact that has a positive effect throughout the school. Schools that value teamwork understand that student success is tied to how well the school's team members work collaboratively to make an impact on overall goals. The emphasis on making an impact is what energizes a staff of teachers to be even more effective.

> *Collaborative culture is the key to success. When you look at all the high-ranking countries, their schools have a collaborative culture where teachers have a history of teamwork and cooperation. They form networks and share resources and work together to create innovative practices that produce student achievement.*[10]
>
> **Andreas Schleicher**

> *Education experts will tell you that of all the things that go into improving a school, nothing—not class size, not technology, not length of the school day—pays off more than giving teachers the time for peer review and constructive feedback, exposure to the best teaching, and time to deepen their knowledge of what they are teaching.*[11]
>
> **Thomas Friedman**

Teachers Are Students of Each Other

There are ways that a culture of collaboration, camaraderie, and cooperation can be instituted at a school. The first step is commitment. To get teachers to commit, they must connect. Start with an induction program for teachers where they get a feeling of belonging.

Experiences of **Harvard's Business School** and **McKinsey's Academy** have shown learning happens best when learners collaborate and help one another. Knowledge is social in nature. School should be a warm, positive place where both teachers and students learn—to speak better, to read better, to solve problems. Cooperation and collaboration are the values students need to go forth into the world to fulfill their destinies.

Researchers have shown that the main reason students in the United States do not perform as well as many of their international peers on achievement measures in math and science is that their teachers are not given the kinds of opportunities to learn from each other. The research shows that it is the collective experience of teachers as they learn from each other that matters most for improving student achievement.[12] Another study found that peer learning among small groups of teachers seems to be the most powerful predictor of student achievement over time.[13]

The problem in the United States is that the rhetoric in education is obsessed with the myth of individuality and the continuing talk of individualized, personalized, and differentiated learning where students work alone on what they want to learn at their own rate of speed.

John Hattie's research shows that individualized instruction has a low effect size of 0.23 (0.40 is the tipping point), showing the negative effects of individualizing instruction. Individualized instruction deprives students of the opportunity to build collaboration with classmates in the classroom, a model that will be required in most work-world settings.

> *Building the group's collective capacity to achieve schoolwide goals must become a higher priority than the individual's independent learning.*[14]
>
> **Rick Dufour**

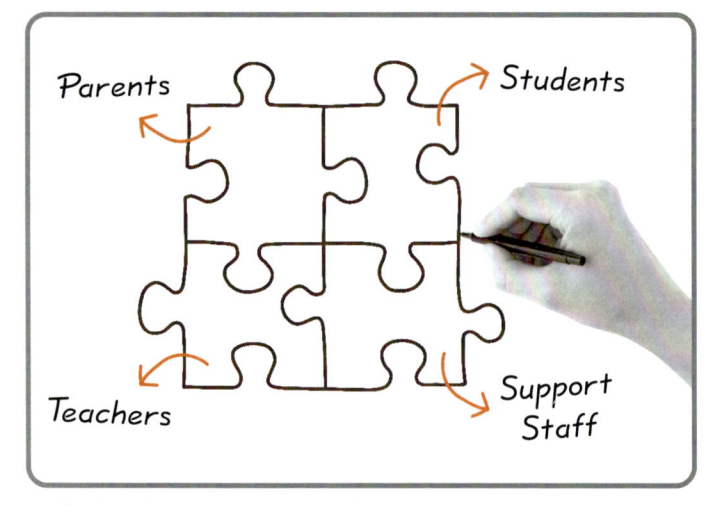

Each piece is an integral part of a school's collective capacity.

Students do not want lessons that are personalized. High-performing countries have shown that when students work together, they are more likely to develop critical thinking skills, creativity, and mastery of complex content.

Principal's Role in Induction

Teachers are a school's greatest asset. This basic fact cannot be repeated often enough. The more schools invest in building the capacity of teachers, the more constructive their output will be. Capacity building is the process by which school administrators improve the skills, knowledge, and other resources of teachers so that they can do their jobs competently. **Improving student achievement is directly linked to the effectiveness of teachers.**

> The responsibility of school administrators is to hire, develop, and support the talent of its teachers.

Administrators must recognize the importance of professional development to establish, nourish, and disseminate the culture of the school. A successful induction program brings order and vision to the process of developing and supporting the capabilities of teachers. An induction program acculturates each new teacher who joins the district's "family" so that the culture of the district is continuously nourished.

Culture is defined by the practices and values of a group. The success of a group is determined by its practices and values. What people do and what they believe will drive an organization. Teachers stay with such a school district because they are part of a common culture where everyone is working toward the same goals.

Teachers will stay with a district when they feel they are valued and add to the culture of the organization.

Improving teacher instructional effectiveness is the most critical factor in improving student achievement and closing the achievement gap. There is not a single teacher who does not know that setting up positive relationships with students is the hallmark of a successful classroom.

But what happens when there are no processes in place for setting up constructive relationships with staff members?

In many schools, the only thing staff members have in common is the parking lot. New teacher induction programs are effective because they are comprehensive, coherent, and continuous.

- **Comprehensive.** There is an organized program consisting of many people, activities, and components, including administrators and the school-site principal.
- **Coherent.** The various components, activities, and people are logically connected to each other.
- **Continuous.** The comprehensive and coherent program continues for many years.

Fundamentals for Impact

In a paper presented to the **American Educational Research Association**, researchers reported that after working with 1,027 teachers, they found that teachers learned more in teacher networks and study groups than with mentoring and that longer, sustained, and intensive professional development programs made a greater impact than shorter ones.[15]

> *I once had a principal who knew how to teach.*
>
> *When you have leadership like this, it produces effective teachers.*
>
> **A teacher**

Effective school administrators know teaching. They know the curriculum. They know instruction. They know to ask, "What exactly do I want to accomplish?" People who do not know what is to be accomplished will adopt programs or buy the latest technology expecting the program or technology to do the teaching of the students—with little input from the classroom teacher.

> *If you want to be an administrator, you've got to understand instruction first. You've got to understand teaching and learning.*
>
> *That's where you have to hang your hat. That's where you get your credibility with teachers.*[16]
>
> **Elaine Farris**
> **Former Kentucky Superintendent**

Schools that do best in improving student achievement are those that have a clear idea of what kind of instructional practice they want to produce, and then design a structure to go with it. In high-performing school systems, principals are promoted from within the profession after they have shown that they can get teachers to work collaboratively with other teachers.

LEADERSHIP
Leading people to work with others to achieve a goal.

In a school where teachers get support, feedback, and the collective stimulation of colleagues influenced by knowledgeable school and district leadership, they keep on growing and developing their capacity to better themselves, their delivery of the instruction, and their rapport with their colleagues and their students.

Thomas Guskey and **Michael Huberman**[17] report that two teachers working together collaboratively raise their productivity by 75 percent and the quality of their work by even more.

> Mentoring is concerned with the individual.
>
> Induction is concerned with the community.

Together **E**veryone **A**chieves **M**ore

They Box Up Everything When They Retire

It's a tragedy. When teachers retire or leave a school, they take everything with them and leave nothing behind. So, when a new teacher comes aboard, that teacher has nothing to reference and has to start all over again at square one. There is no file, no box, no notes, no thumb drive of photos, lessons, posters, pictures—nothing. You would think that if all of the past teachers would have left copies of their lesson plans, activities, and tests, new teachers would have a body of past experience and information to access. That seldom happens.

Worse yet, the school often has a mismatched set of concepts that are labeled curriculum guides. Beginning teachers usually have to ask for these items as they have been boxed up and carted away with the departing teacher's belongings.

Ruth was a good teacher who taught for thirty-seven years. When she retired, there was no protocol or tradition for her to share what she had accumulated during her tenure. No one asked if she would leave behind what she had collected to be shared with the other teachers or the new teachers coming in. There was no exit interview. There was no opportunity to pass along the culture of an effective classroom teacher to others.

While Ruth did not leave her legacy at her school, she did ship her years of wisdom to a university that shared it with a group preservice teachers who gladly availed themselves of the treasures.

Building A Community

"The district's culture, mission, and beliefs are shared during the induction program to newly employed teachers when they join the family. If this is not done then, when do you?"[18]

Joan Hearne, retired
Professional Development Director
Wichita, Kansas

Novice teachers want teachers they can watch teach in their rooms, teachers who will give them activities and lesson plans, teachers who will tell them what to do with those students who challenge even the best in the field. We dignify the teaching profession when teachers teach other teachers.

Teachers today come into education from a social world and are eager to engage and cooperate. They eat at communal tables in restaurants and meet each other on the Internet. Induction immediately fosters and continues an integrated professional culture. New teachers want to learn; they are willing to contribute; they are eager to help make a difference. Most importantly, they want to belong to a community of learners. An induction program enables new teachers to begin teaching on day one with the knowledge that they are an integral part of their school, and it enables them to continue contributing to the knowledge base of both teachers and students throughout their tenure.

Shared beliefs are the core feature of collaborative impact, and these beliefs are shared with new teachers when they join the staff. Numerous studies show that when schools value professional collaboration and have a set of shared beliefs, there will be an impact on student achievement.[19, 20, 21]

It is better to train a teacher and lose that teacher, than to not train a teacher and keep that teacher.

Done well, induction to the profession can strengthen schools as well as teachers. Novice teachers represent the future of education. They are the next generation of leaders. The nourishment they receive through a comprehensive induction program will help them grow into excellent effective classroom veterans.

> **The ultimate purpose of any school is the success and achievement of its students.**

A new teacher's success will determine the success of an entire generation of students. Those who develop into effective teachers have students who will make dramatic achievement gains.

"If you had a good teacher five years in a row, you could completely make up for the difference between low-income and middle-income achievement."[22]

Eric Hanushek
Stanford University

Teaching is a highly skilled craft, one that requires a systematic, sustained, and relentless process of training and support to produce a retained skill.

> **When teachers work together, the impact they have on student learning and achievement is undeniable.**

The teacher is the most significant influence on student achievement. It makes total sense to train teachers to be effective from the very start of their careers.

Endnotes

[1] Madeline Will, "How Bad Is the Teacher Shortage? What Two New Studies Say," *Education Week* (September 6, 2022): https://www.edweek.org/leadership/how-bad-is-the-teacher-shortage-what-two-new-studies-say/2022/09.

[2] Laura Pomerance and Kate Walsh, *2020 Teacher Prep Review: Clinical Practice and Classroom Management* (Washington, DC: National Council on Teacher Quality, 2020).

[3] John Hattie, *Visible Learning: A Synthesis of Over 800 Meta-Analyses Relating to Achievement* (New York: Routledge, 2009).

[4] "Hattie Ranking: 256 Influences and Effect Sizes Related to Student Achievement," *Visible Learning*, accessed July 1, 2023, https://visible-learning.org/backup-hattie-ranking-256-effects-2017/.

[5] Simon Gibbs and Ben Powell, "Teacher Efficacy and Pupil Behaviour: The Structure of Teachers' Individual and Collective Beliefs and Their Relationship with Numbers of Pupils Excluded from School," *British Journal of Educational Psychology* 82 (December 2012): 564–584.

[6] Hattie, *Visible Learning*.

[7] Joan Richardson, "The Editor's Note: Getting Better at Learning," *Phi Delta Kappan* 98, no. 3 (October 31, 2016): 4.

[8] Hattie, *Visible Learning*.

[9] Eric A. Hanushek, "Focus on Teaching, Not Just Masks and Hand-Sanitizer: Make Schools Better Than They Were by Relying More on the Best Teachers," *Education Next* (Fall, 2021).

[10] Andreas Schleicher, "Collaborative Culture Is the Key to Success," *Times Educational Supplement* (March 8, 2013).

[11] Thomas L. Friedman, "The Shanghai Secret," *The New York Times*, October 22, 2013.

[12] J. Stigler and J. Hiebert, "Closing the Teaching Gap," *Phi Delta Kappan* 91, no. 3 (November 2009): 32–37.

[13] C. K. Jackson and E. Bruegmann, "Teaching Students and Teaching Each Other: The Importance of Peer Learning for Teachers," *American Economic Journal: Applied Economics* 1, no. 4 (October 2009): 85–108.

[14] Richard DuFour and Timothy Berkey, "The Principal as Staff Developer," *Journal of Staff Development* 16, no. 4 (Fall 1995).

[15] Michael Garet, A. Porter, L. Desmoine, B. Birman, and S. K. Kwang, "What Makes Professional Development Effective?" *American Educational Research Journal* 38, no. 4 (December 2001): 915–945.

[16] Autumn A. Arnett, "Kentucky's First Black Superintendent Reflects on Her Journey and 'Mastery for Every Child' Education Philosophy," *Education Dive* (February 26, 2018).

[17] Thomas R. Guskey and Michael Huberman, eds., *Professional Development in Education: New Paradigms and Practices* (New York: Teachers College Press, 1995).

[18] From an email communication between Harry Wong and Joan Hearne.

[19] Jenni Donohoo and Steven Katz, "What Drives Collective Efficacy?" *Educational Leadership* 76, no. 9 (July 1, 2019).

[20] John Hattie, "High-Impact Leadership," *Educational Leadership* 72, no. 5 (February 2015): 36–40.

[21] Roger Goddard, Wayne Hoy, and Anita Woolfolk Hoy, "Collective Teacher Efficacy: Its Meaning, Measure, and Impact on Student Achievement," *American Educational Research Journal* 37, no. 2 (January 2000): 479–507.

[22] Eric A. Hanushek, "An Interview: High Quality Education: Elements and Implications," https://childrenofthecode.org/interviews/hanushek.htm.

Mentoring Is Not Induction

Mentoring is haphazard and individual; induction is collaborative and collegial.

Mentoring vs. Induction

The literature is filled with such terms as "induction and mentoring" or "induction/mentoring." The inference is that induction and mentoring are one and the same, or that if you give a teacher a mentor, you have done all you need to do to induct a teacher into the profession.

> The terms induction and mentoring are often incorrectly used interchangeably.

Induction and mentoring **are not** the same. Induction is an organized, sustained program structured by a school or district to develop effective teachers. In contrast, mentoring is what one person, called a mentor, does and is often carried out in isolation.

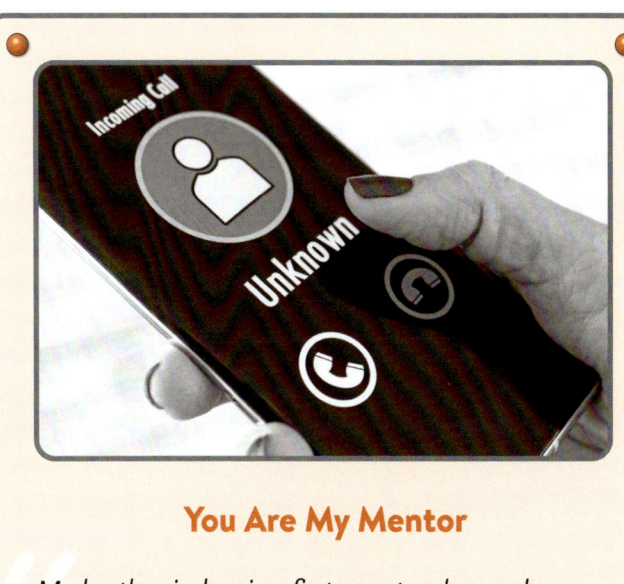

You Are My Mentor

My brother-in-law is a first-year teacher and was having a horrible time. The district provided no induction program and when he asked for help, he was told to contact his mentor. He didn't even know he had a mentor. So, he called this teacher and informed her that she was his mentor.

She questioned, "I am?" He said, "Thanks, but no thanks," and hung up.

The May 4, 2021, issue of *Education Week* published an article, "Mentors Matter for New Teachers,"[1] that stated **MENTORS SHOULD BE IMPARTIAL GUIDES BY THE SIDE AND THAT TEACHERS SHOULD CHOOSE THEIR OWN GOALS**. These recommendations were made in bold print and emphasized with capital letters. Can you imagine flying on a plane knowing that the pilot has only had a "guide-by-the-side" and can fly the plane as she or he pleases?

The article also stated that 92 percent of new teachers who receive a mentor return to teaching the following year. There is no research to substantiate this claim. In fact, numerous researchers such as **Susan Wynn** at Duke University have found that there is no relationship between mentoring and teacher retention.[2]

Would you take a flight knowing that the only training the pilot received was from a mentor?

The Great Tragedy of Mentoring

In many schools, all a new teacher gets for help is a mentor who has received no training in how to help new teachers and may only be available to help if asked. The mentor is a "safety net" responding to a new teacher's day-to-day crises and providing quick, survival teaching tips that do not create a connection between well-executed professional learning communities and student learning.

What new teachers never see with a mentor or a "guide-by-the-side" are the organizing strategies experienced teachers use to plan, design, manage, and pace a lesson. New teachers never see the advance work and classroom management strategies that the master teacher uses during the first few days of school to set the tone for a positive learning environment.

The novice teacher only sees the outcome of a smoothly functioning lesson—but never sees the strategy that went into the development of the veteran teacher's lesson planning processes. In Japan, a new teacher sees these strategies when they are involved in a group's lesson study. In Finland, teachers are didacticians, people who can create the necessary conditions for learning, but new teachers never see or learn this process when they turn to a mentor for survival, rather than learn how to be proficient. (See the rubric on page 106.)

"How am I doing" often leaves the teacher with no answer or direction.

With a mentor, the new teacher never sees active planning, the pulling together of materials and resources for the lesson. They never see the bigger picture and how veteran teachers plan backwards from the end of the unit. During instructional planning, veteran teachers make decisions on the basis of the learner, asking the question, "Who are my learners?" And if necessary, "How do I make last minute adjustments to change the lesson on the fly based on lesson assessment?"

With a mentor, new teachers never get an answer to "How am I doing?" because a mentor lets the new teachers choose their own goals.

The Problem with Mentors

Many mentors are not trained. Teachers often volunteer to be mentors for the extra money they are given for the role. The principal is not involved in monitoring or assessing the mentoring process. The mentor rarely reports to the principal and each person mentors in his or her own way—even if it's ineffective—so that if you have ten new teachers, the result will be ten teachers getting ten different approaches.

Mentors see their role as helping new teachers survive; they do not see that it is their role and responsibility to develop teachers who can perform effectively.

This is the problem with most mentors.

- They receive no training.
- They are selected because they have experience over proficiency.
- They apply for the work to get additional pay.
- There is no curriculum or set of goals to which they mentor.
- They seldom report to the principal to share progress.
- They rarely interact with other mentors.
- They are given no schedule or allocated time and not told what to do or when to do it.
- They do not teach specific classroom management or instructional skills; rather, they mentor by answering questions for immediate relief.

> *New teachers are given so little support in my district that they are simply doomed to fail. Yet no one notices, and they finish their probationary status without a negative evaluation.*
>
> A teacher

The use of mentors is a remarkably narrow process. One-on-one mentoring often lacks real structure, simply relying on the willingness of the veteran and the new teacher to seek out each other. Many mentors just respond to a new teacher's day-to-day problems and provide survival teaching tips. They are simply a safety net for the new teachers. Mentoring fails to create a connection between well-executed professional learning communities and student learning. **There is no school culture, and collaborative practices are not fostered.**

The Lack of Rigorous Research

There is no research to validate the effectiveness of mentoring. Only in education do we talk about "mentoring alone" as sufficient for induction. What's unsettling about this attitude is that it has become institutionalized.

> **Repeated research reports that mentoring as a strategy has not worked.**

In an *ERIC Digest*, **Sharon Feiman-Nemser**[3] shared the findings of forty years of research on mentoring and its effectiveness.

- Claims about mentoring have not been subjected to rigorous empirical scrutiny.
- Few comprehensive studies exist that have examined in depth the context, content, and consequences of mentoring.
- We are jeopardizing an entire generation of new teachers with a process that has not produced any systematic results.

MENTORING ≠ RESULTS

Chapter 3: Mentoring Is Not Induction • 27

The Myth of Mentors

For twenty years, almost every time an article appears where there is a discussion about using mentors, we have made these simple requests of the authors.

- Can you share a randomized, controlled experiment that shows the efficacy of mentoring?
- Can you share a district or school that has used mentors to produce effective new teachers? How can their model be replicated?

We have never received a response, yet the education press continues to recommend mentors as its model to produce effective new teachers. This is despite the glaring, research-based fact that **mentors have never been shown to improve new teacher effectiveness**.

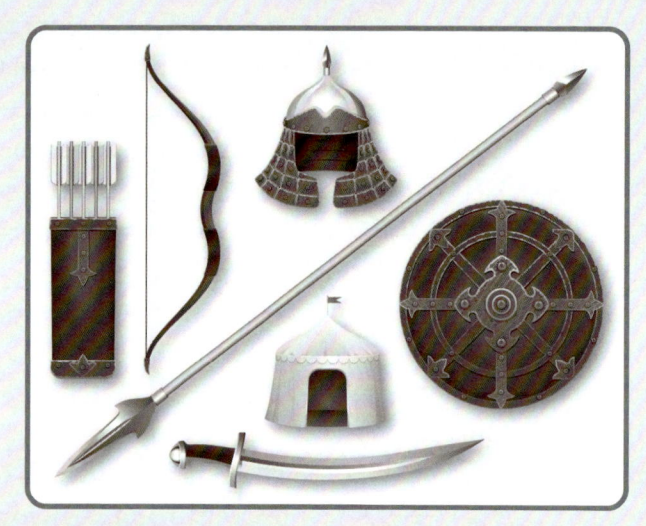

Mentors can be likened to the Mamluks. The Mamluks knew *furusiyya*, mounted warfare using the bow, lance, and saber. The Egyptians ruled the world for three hundred years using their skills. But gunpowder began to be used in warfare and, in 1556, the Mamluks were disastrously defeated, and Egypt became a province of the Ottoman empire. The Mamluks had stuck to their old ways, resisting change and progress.

The analogy to the American educational system is striking. It continues to flounder and bluster its way with mentors when it has been clear for a decade or more that the system is inadequate and there are better ways to conduct professional development, clearly exemplified by how high-performing countries induct their new teachers into the profession.

Other researchers have found that mentoring alone is not a proven strategy.

- Over one million new teachers received mentoring over a ten-year period and outcomes found that little is known about the benefits teachers may have received, how the impact of mentoring varies across different types of programs, and its effects on teacher and student outcomes.[4]

- Mentor programs harm more than help first-year teachers. Instead of helping beginning teachers, mentors tend to reinforce the status quo, making it difficult for teachers to promote a deep understanding of teaching.[5]

- Current research does not yet provide definitive evidence of the value of mentoring programs in keeping new teachers from leaving the profession.[6]

- Mentoring is not helpful in and of itself.[7]

- New teachers' needs are so varied and immediate that expertise and experience is unlikely to reside in one mentor who is available when needed.[8]

- Mentoring cannot be done adequately by another teacher with a full-time load who drops by when time permits or when a problem arises.[9]

- The millions of dollars consumed and spent on mentoring programs would be better spent on fostering collegial learning with existing teams of teachers and the next generation of new teachers.[10]

- For too many teachers, the mentoring pairing process results in a "blind date." The teachers do not know each other and neither partner has input into the pairing.[11]

- Mentoring has, at best, been a poorly designed and ineffectively implemented interaction between the mentor and the mentee. Far too many new teachers experience a disillusioning relationship that provides little support during this crucial stage of their career.[12]

- It is well documented that there is little empirical evidence to support specific mentoring practices.[13, 14, 15]

- The mere presence of a guide does not improve teaching. Mentoring by itself is not enough to retain and develop teachers. Mentoring programs vary widely and may do little more than ask mentors to check in with new teachers a few times per semester to chat.[16]

- Mentoring, in and of itself, has no purpose, goal, or agenda for student achievement. Thus, mentoring alone fails to provide evidence of the connection between well-executed professional learning communities and student learning.[17]

- The truth is that mentoring pairs seldom are anything but haphazard. Rarely are mentors people who really know the subject that the individual is teaching.[18]

- Many mentoring programs lack key pedagogical content and the structural characteristics of effective professional development that are needed to produce effective teachers.[19]

- Negative outcomes have been reported, such that unstructured buddy mentoring can have harmful results and can actually be worse than no mentoring at all.[20]

- Many programs provide brief mentor training and/or orientation for mentors and mentees and then send them on their way with little or no ongoing support.[21]

- New teachers were more likely to receive superficial support than support that might help improve their skills and knowledge of instructional techniques and classroom management, such as observing their mentor or having their mentor demonstrate a lesson.[22]

- Research has not been found that supports the systematic formation of effective teachers solely through the use of mentors, especially mentors who show up after school begins and may not have been trained, compensated, or given direction or goals to attain.[23]

- Districts and schools would do better to rely less on one-on-one mentoring and instead develop schoolwide structures that promote integrated professional cultures with frequent exchange of information and ideas across experience levels.[24]

- The Swiss philosophy explicitly rejects a "deficit" model that new teachers need mentors. Instead, there is a carefully crafted array of induction experiences for new teachers.[25]

- A poorly prepared or over-extended mentor can be of little assistance, and, in some situations where mentor selection is haphazard, mentors may even reinforce bad practice.[26]

The conclusion is simple. **Simply assigning a mentor does not produce improved student achievement or remedy the situation of teachers becoming discouraged and leaving the profession.** A mentor, in and of itself, has no purpose, goal, or agenda for student achievement. The technique is not sustainable or replicable, and there is little administrative support or involvement when a mentor is used.

After a year of one-on-one mentoring, the new teacher retreats to the practice of stand-alone teaching in an isolated classroom.

Tutoring and Coaching

In Greek legend, **Mentor** was the faithful friend of Odysseus (Ulysses), the hero of *The Odyssey*.

When Odysseus went to fight the Trojans, he instructed Mentor to be teacher and adviser to his son, Telemachus. Thus, Mentor was not just a mere mentor. His role was to impart wisdom based on experience.

Unfortunately, much educational literature describes a mentor as a facilitator or support person. A new teacher needs wisdom based on classroom experience.

Districts continue to pour millions of dollars into one-on-one mentoring programs. There is no consistency with one-on-one mentoring. As a process, it cannot be duplicated. It is a random, hit-or-miss system and, for the most part, totally inadequate. That is the problem.

If your child needs help with a subject, such as math, you enlist the services of a tutor who will teach your child the necessary skills to succeed in math. A tutor is an expert in a particular field who is trained to impart knowledge, skills, and acquired wisdom.

The coach of a sports team determines how the team is to play. Coaches and tutors in education teach and advise. They instruct and work with teachers to prepare and develop their skills so that they are able to perform at their peak.

> **The key word in coaching and tutoring is performance.**
>
> **The key word in mentoring is survival.**

Every team begins the new season with a training period so players understand "how WE do things here." Likewise, an induction process should be used to improve new teacher performance and show new teachers "how WE do things here."

A Comparison	
Mentors	**Coaches and Tutors**
Are available for survival and support	Help teachers improve student learning
Provide emotional support; answer singular procedural questions	Coach to improve instructional performance on a sustained basis
Have reflective conversations	Focus on student learning strategies and techniques
Treat mentoring as an isolated activity	Part job-embedded induction and staff development process
Just a buddy	Have a leadership responsibility
Report to no one	Report to the principal

The ideal time to utilize coaches and tutors with new teachers is when they are eager to improve their performance. Administrators and high-performing teachers welcome coaches and tutors as they seek to expand their horizons and skills.

- Coaches and tutors help teachers articulate what it is they want to accomplish and then help them reach those goals.
- Coaches and tutors ask probing questions so teachers can master their skills and improve their performance.
- Coaches and tutors model and demonstrate effective practices.
- Coaches and tutors offer assessment (non-evaluative) feedback on a regular basis.
- Coaches and tutors encourage continuous learning to develop successful practices.

Coaching is an ongoing process, as open-ended as our desire for continuous improvement.

New Teachers Want to Succeed

New teachers want more than a job. They want to make a difference. They want to experience success. They don't want to work in isolation. They want to contribute to a group. The best induction programs provide connection because they are structured within learning communities where new and veteran teachers interact and treat each other with respect and are valued for their respective contributions.

> *I never sat in anyone else's classroom even once. Mine is the only teaching style I know. I felt that sometimes I was reinventing the wheel.*
>
> Gail A. Saborio
> Rhode Island

Effective school districts have a superintendent, director of professional development, a new teacher induction leader, or a principal who determines what new teachers need to be taught to be successful and effective.

It is incumbent that administrators and policy makers create schools with a culture where collaborative impact is focused on pursuing a common vision for student learning.

Knowledgeable administrators and staff developers know that teachers learn best from watching others teach. Thus, many induction programs have model classrooms where neophyte teachers can visit and learn in networks and collegial sessions. In high-performing countries (Chapter 8), new teachers are tutored, coached, and supervised.

> Learning together helps us make better choices for ourselves.

Michael Garet and others, from a study with 1,027 public school math and science teachers in kindergarten through grade 12, reported that teachers learn more

- in teacher networks and study groups than with mentoring,
- in professional development programs that are longer, sustained, and more intensive than shorter ones,
- when there is collective participation, and
- when they perceive teacher learning and development as part of the coherent professional development program.[27]

Good teaching thrives when teachers feel that they are connected to their schools and colleagues. This is only possible when there is a strong culture of collaboration.

> **In an effective induction program, there is a clear understanding that high-quality teaching and strong student performance require robust, collaborative, professional development opportunities that are job-embedded and teacher-led.**

Lack of Leadership

In the United States, there is a serious lack of leadership in education. There is no process to bring teachers together and develop the instructional capacity of its teachers. Teachers are at the mercy of the latest fleeting pronouncement.

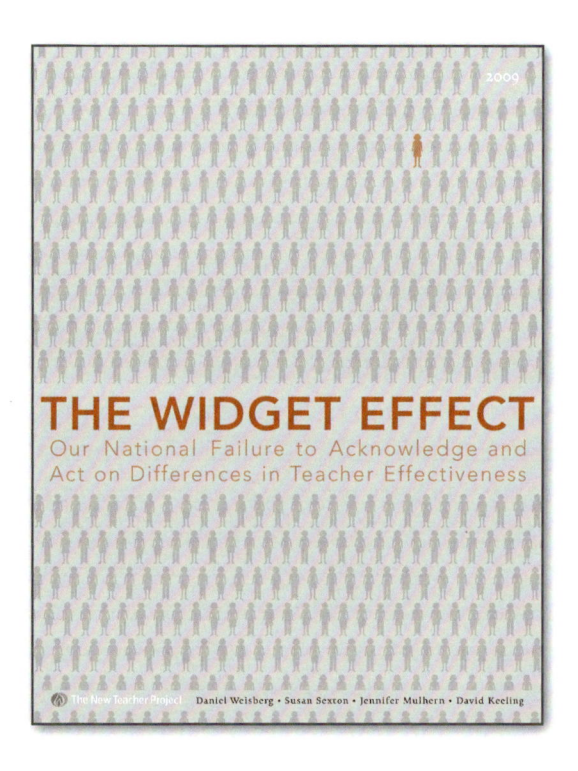

In 2009, **The New Teacher Project** published a document, "The Widget Effect," showing that teachers are treated as widgets—people who are moved around in a haphazard fashion to fulfill the latest fad, approach, or what is politically expedient. The great tragedy is that the teaching profession of over 3.5 million members has allowed this to happen to them.

There are bad teachers. We know that. There are also bad schools, but there is a difference between a bad teacher and a bad school. Bad teachers yearn for help at the end of every day because they know instinctively that there must be better ways to teach more effectively.

Bad schools, however, have a constant churn of superintendents and principals who do not seem to know that there are better ways to manage schools. They do not share a coherent, explicit set of norms and expectations about what good schools look like. They aren't rational enough to know that improvement has to do with the beliefs and practices that teachers in the school share. It is not in the next program or technology that is adopted. The people who administrate low-performing schools don't know what to do or how to do it. If they did, they would be doing it.

You can't improve a school's performance, or that of any teacher or student in it, without increasing the investment in teachers' knowledge, pedagogical skills, and understanding of students.

Teacher success translates into student success.

Induct Your Teachers and They Will Stay

Harvard economist **Ronald Ferguson** studied 900 Texas school districts and concluded that every additional dollar spent on developing more highly effective teachers resulted in greater increases in student achievement than other, non-instructional uses of school resources.[28]

> The most cost-effective way to increase student achievement is to improve teacher performance instead of providing another quick-fix program or providing a mentor.

An induction process is the best way to send a message to new teachers that you value them and want them to succeed and stay.

To reiterate, simply giving a new teacher a mentor has no research-backed validity. Instead, invest in an induction program that will retain new teachers and help them become better and more effective teachers. The gain—to taxpayers, schools, educators, students, and communities—is immense.

Every new teacher is a human resource—a person who has invested years in preparing for a life dedicated to helping young people. We have a responsibility to ensure that these new teachers will learn and succeed, just as we have a responsibility to ensure that every student will learn and succeed.

Endnotes

[1] Elizabeth Heubeck, "Mentors Matter for New Teachers. Advice on What Works and Doesn't," *Education Week* (May 4, 2021): 22.

[2] Susan Wynn, Lisa Carboni, and Erika Patall, "Beginning Teachers' Perceptions of Mentoring, Climate, and Leadership: Promoting Retention Through a Learning Communities Perspective," *Leadership and Policy in Schools* 6, no. 3 (2007): 209–229.

[3] Sharon Feiman-Nemser, "Teacher Mentoring: A Critical Review," *ERIC Digest* (July 1996).

[4] Jonah Rockoff, "Does Mentoring Reduce Turnover and Improve Skills of New Employees? Evidence from Teachers in New York City," NBER Working Paper, (March 2008).

[5] Iowa State University, "Mentor Programs Harm, More Than Help New Teachers," *ScienceDaily* (April 21, 2014): https://www.sciencedaily.com/releases/2014/04/140421135538.htm.

[6] Richard Ingersoll and Jeffrey Kralik, "The Impact of Mentoring on Teacher Retention: What the Research Says," *The Education Commission of the States* (January 2004): 15.

[7] Zewelanji Serpell and Leslie A. Bozeman, *Beginning Teacher Induction: A Report on Beginning Teacher Effectiveness and Retention* (Washington, DC: National Partnership for Excellence and Accountability in Teaching, 1999).

[8] Mark Schlager, Judith Fusco, Melissa Koch, Valerie Crawford, and Michelle Phillips, "Designing Equity and Diversity Into Online Strategies to Support New Teachers," *National Educational Computing Conference*, Washington State Convention and Trade Center, Seattle Conference Presentation (2003).

[9] Paul R. Lehman, "Ten Steps to School Reform at Bargain Prices," *Education Week* (November 26, 2003).

[10] Thomas R. Guskey and Michael Huberman, eds., *Professional Development in Education: New Paradigms and Practices* (New York: Teachers College Press, 1995).

[11] Jon Saphier, Susan Freedman, and Barbara Aschheim, *Beyond Mentoring: Comprehensive Induction Programs: How to Attract, Support and Retain New Teachers* (Newton, MA: Teachers 21, 2001).

[12] J. Boreen and D. Niday, *Mentoring Across Boundaries* (Portland, ME: Stenhouse Publishers, 2003).

[13] C. Bennetts, "Lifelong Learners: In Their Own Words," *International Journal of Lifelong Education* 20, no. 4 (2001): 272–288.

[14] P. Hawk, "Beginning Teacher Programs: Benefits for the Experienced Educator," *Action in Teacher Education* 8, no. 4 (1986–1987): 59–63.

[15] J. Little, "The Mentor Phenomenon and the Social Organization of Teaching," in C. B. Cazden, ed., *Review of Research in Education* (Washington, DC: American Educational Research Association, 1990): 297–351.

[16] Alliance for Excellent Education, "Tapping the Potential: Retaining and Developing High Quality New Teachers" (Washington, DC: Alliance for Excellent Education, 2004): 13.

[17] E. Britton, L. Paine, S. Raizen, and D. Pimm, *Comprehensive Teacher Induction: Systems for Early Career Learning* (Kluwer Academic Publishers and WestEd, 2003): https://www.WestEd.org.

[18] Susan Moore Johnson, Sarah E. Birkeland, Susan M. Kardos, David Kauffman, Edward Liu, and Heather G. Peske, "Retaining the Next Generation of Teachers: The Importance of School Based Support," *Harvard Education Letter* (2001).

[19] S. Gordon and S. Maxey, *How to Help Beginning Teachers Succeed, 2nd edition* (Arlington, VA: ASCD, 2000).

[20] F. Head et al., *The Reality of Mentoring: Complexity in Its Process and Function* (Reston, VA: Association of Teacher Educators, 1992).

[21] A. Lewis, "School Reform and Professional Development," *Phi Delta Kappan* 83, no. 7 (2002).

[22] P. Shields et al., *The Status of the Teaching Profession 2003. Teaching and California's Future* (Santa Cruz, CA: The Center for the Future of Teaching and Learning, 2003).

[23] M. Schmoker, quoted in A. Breaux and H. Wong, *New Teacher Induction: How to Train, Support, and Retain New Teachers* (Mountain View, CA: Harry K. Wong Publications, 2003): 55.

[24] Susan Moore Johnson and Sarah E. Birkeland, "Pursuing a Sense of Success: New Teachers Explain Their Career Decisions," *American Educational Research Journal* (Fall 2003): 608.

[25] Harry Wong, Ted Britton, and Tom Ganser, "What the World Can Teach Us About New Teacher Induction," *Phi Delta Kappan* 86, no. 5 (January 2005): 379–384.

[26] Kathleen Fulton, Irene Yoon, and Christine Lee, "Induction Into Learning Communities," National Commission on Teaching and America's Future (August 2005).

[27] Michael S. Garet, Andrew C. Porter, Laura Desimone, Beatrice F. Birman, and Kwang Suk Yoon, "What Makes Professional Development Effective? Results from a National Sample of Teachers," *American Educational Research Journal* (January 2001).

[28] Ronald F. Ferguson, "Paying for Public Education: New Evidence on How and Why Money Matters," *Harvard Journal of Legislation* 28 (Summer 1991): 465–498.

Induction Programs That Retain and Develop

4 **A School with No Attrition**
There is little attrition in a school where everyone works together with common goals and expectations. 37

5 **Moberly School District**
Teachers stay when there is a school culture of collaboration, consistency, and continuity. 41

6 **Flowing Wells Unified School District**
When teachers succeed, students succeed. 45

7 **The Stay Interview**
A stay interview is a dialogue, a conversation, not an evaluation of a teacher's performance. 52

4   A School with No Attrition

There is little attrition in a school where everyone works together with common goals and expectations.

No Teacher Attrition

Bridget Phillips

For the past thirty years, **Bridget Phillips**, a principal in Clark County, Nevada, has helped new teachers succeed in the classroom. Her school has a vulnerable population—students from an impoverished, highly service-oriented community. **But her school has no new teacher attrition.**

Posted in every classroom, the hallways, the library, and the cafeteria is a **"Success Trail"** poster that spells out the way the school operates.

Getting Teachers to Stay

Research findings suggest that the most effective teachers tend to stay in teaching and in specific schools. In fact, the more effective teachers are *less* likely to leave their schools or the profession.[1]

The research did not find evidence that more effective teachers were more likely to leave challenging contexts.

On the contrary. They were willing and able to achieve success with students, no matter what the context and the difficulties they encountered.

What does this suggest?

Train your teachers to be successful and they will stay, no matter what the context.

Teachers stay when they work successfully together.

Chapter 4: A School with No Attrition • 37

The Success Trail poster reminds everyone of the schoolwide procedures in place.

- Morning Procedures
- Hall Procedures
- Lunchroom Procedures
- Dismissal Procedures
- Bathroom Procedures, and more

When new teachers come to teach at Bridget's school, a culture of success is already evident. The teachers help each other, and even the students themselves teach the schoolwide and classroom procedures to the new teachers and any substitute teachers.

I Can't Believe the Difference

❝*In my twelve years of teaching, this is the first school I've been in where the entire staff has bought into the idea of common procedures for making the beginning of the school year successful. I can't believe the difference it has made from other beginnings I have experienced. From day one everyone had common goals and expectations. It's been wonderful here!*

Shaunene Chandia
Teacher

What New Teachers Are Taught

- How things are done
- The curriculum to teach
- The instruction to use
- A vision of student achievement

Bridget takes all of her first-year teachers through an in-house induction training program for one semester. A cadre of administrators and teachers teach the induction program. The purpose of this training is to support and retain effective teachers.

In the second semester, student teachers from the local university assigned to her school are taken through a very similar training induction program. This exposes them to an array of master teachers, rather than the traditional one-on-one pairing with a mentor. If a vacancy is expected at the school, Bridget can invite one of these preservice teachers to join her staff before the teacher applies for a job elsewhere. As an active trainer in the induction process, Bridget is scouting the talent, ready to draft should the need arise.

Even more impressive, if one of the student teachers is hired as a regular teacher, that first-year teacher goes through the same first-year induction program at the start of the school year given to all beginning teachers. Student teachers and new teachers are surveyed as to their needs. The list is publicized, and more experienced teachers respond with willingness to answer, help, or present sessions at in-house training meetings. This is a true learning community of educators sharing with and helping fellow educators.

When it comes to teacher retention, research says that supportive leadership is the number one factor found to be "absolutely essential." Teachers who are satisfied in their jobs stay. With so much at stake, school leaders have a responsibility to cultivate a culture that supports teachers, meets their needs, and develops their skills.

Study after study has shown that most new teachers would forego more money in favor of
- a good principal,
- the chance to work collaboratively with effective teachers, and
- an orderly, focused, and consistent school atmosphere.

The two factors that build a consistent school atmosphere are
1. instructional leadership, and
2. staff members that work collaboratively.

To build capacity and retain experienced teachers, an administrator must be skilled in instruction.

Bridget Phillips has been principal of her school for decades. It's hard to build an effective staff with a revolving door of personnel. Furthermore, when leaders keep changing, schools constantly lurch from one direction to another causing teachers to leave in search of stability.

Worse yet, students start to feel that nobody cares enough to stay and when nobody else cares, neither do they. When there is a culture of high turnover, teachers feel overwhelmed and alone, and they lose hope quickly. Then they leave as well, like the others before them, preserving the very problem that defeated them. What's the solution?

The research of **Susan Moore Johnson** and her colleagues shows that teachers are more likely to stay in their school or the profession if their work occurs in cultures of collaboration.[2] Any effort to provide support, fulfillment, and a growing repertoire of effective strategies for young teachers will increase the likelihood that they will stay and grow into effective teachers.

Clark County Induction Program

The **Clark County School District** in Las Vegas is the fifth largest school district in the United States. They hire between 1,400 to 1,800 new teachers every year and have been able to show a retention rate higher than the national average. In comparison to the national attrition rate of 55 percent, the district has saved an estimated $1,320,000 since the 2014–2015 school year by reducing the attrition of beginning teachers.

Clark County provides its new teachers with a customized induction program known as the **Beginning Teacher Induction Program (BTIP)**. The BTIP consists of a series of professional learning opportunities that are specifically designed to support new teachers throughout their first two years of work and retain them for a life-long career. Many of the professional learning opportunities focus on classroom management, instructional engagement, and building a positive culture and climate.

The induction process is focused on organizing collaborative team opportunities with the theme, "We are centered on the idea that as a larger collective, we can all be greater together."

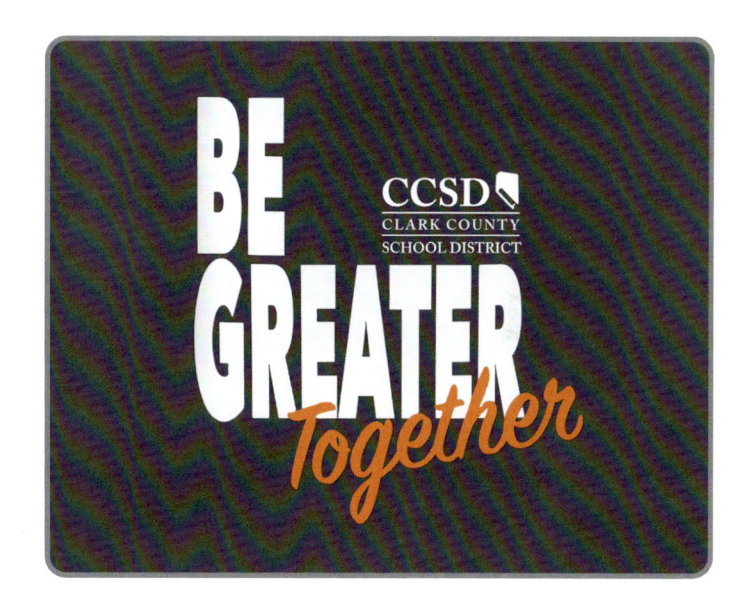

In a typical year, the induction program provides approximately ninety-nine large scale professional learning opportunities. During each professional learning session, instructors demonstrate multiple instructional strategies that new teachers can take back to their classrooms. Through these ongoing induction events, relationships are built that positively impact the new teachers throughout their career to ensure they can "Be Greater Together."

A Greater Part of the Whole

Whether teachers will choose to remain in the profession depends heavily on their experiences during the first critical years in the classroom. **The research is clear that new teachers need to be supported and valued with training and professional development opportunities.** They also need time to collaborate with their peers to ease the feeling of isolation. It is imperative that school systems and schools adapt measures and commit the time and resources necessary to effectively train and support new teachers, in whose hands we so trustingly place the future.

> Individually we are one drop. Together we are an ocean.

Endnotes

[1] Dan Goldhaber, Betheny Gross, and Daniel Player, *Are Public Schools Really Losing Their Best? Assessing the Career Transitions of Teachers and Their Implications for the Quality of the Teacher Workforce* (CALDER Urban Institute, 2007).

[2] S. M. Johnson, M. A. Kraft, and J. P. Papay, "How Context Matters in High-Need Schools: The Effects of Teachers' Working Conditions on Their Professional Satisfaction and Their Students' Achievement," *Teachers College Record* 114, no. 10 (2012): 1–39.

5 Moberly School District

Teachers stay when there is a school culture of collaboration, consistency, and continuity.

Rural Challenges

Roughly half a million U.S. teachers either move or leave the profession each year—attrition that costs the country up to $2.2 billion annually.[1] This high turnover rate disproportionately affects rural and high-poverty schools and seriously compromises the nation's capacity to ensure that all students have access to skilled teaching.

Rural school districts have traditionally been the outlier of education with their long list of challenges—concentrated poverty, inadequate access to health care services, lack of high-quality early childhood education and childcare, difficulty staffing special education and ELL teachers, ballooning class sizes, high transportation costs, teacher shortages, lack of adequate Internet access, and inequitable funding.

There is, however, a rural school district in the "Show Me State" that has no difficulty attracting, hiring, and retaining new teachers.

The Moberly Induction Program

Moberly (population 13,000) is a small rural town in Missouri. In 2008, **Gena McCluskey**, the then assistant superintendent and subsequent superintendent, plucked a middle school teacher, **Tara Link**, to start a new teacher induction program. They named it **S.H.I.N.E.—Supporting, Helping, and Inspiring New Educators**.

Gena McCluskey's motivation to start an induction program stemmed from the fact that every school seemed to be starting over again each year with new, inexperienced teachers, taking two steps forward and three steps backward. She knew there had to be a way to create a system of support and professional development for newly hired classroom teachers when they joined a school so that they would stay and create a culture of collaboration and continuity.

Tara Link

Implementing S.H.I.N.E.

Planning for Your First Year as a Moberly Spartan

- Classroom Management
- Lesson Planning
- Tips for Organizing
- Parent Communication
- Behavior Management
- Positive Expectations
- Professionalism
- Other considerations

The single greatest effect on student achievement is the effectiveness of the teacher.

The Moberly School District in Missouri knows how to prepare and grow its greatest asset—its teachers.

Its program is about **S**upporting, **H**elping, and **I**nspiring **N**ew **E**ducators so they will **S.H.I.N.E.**

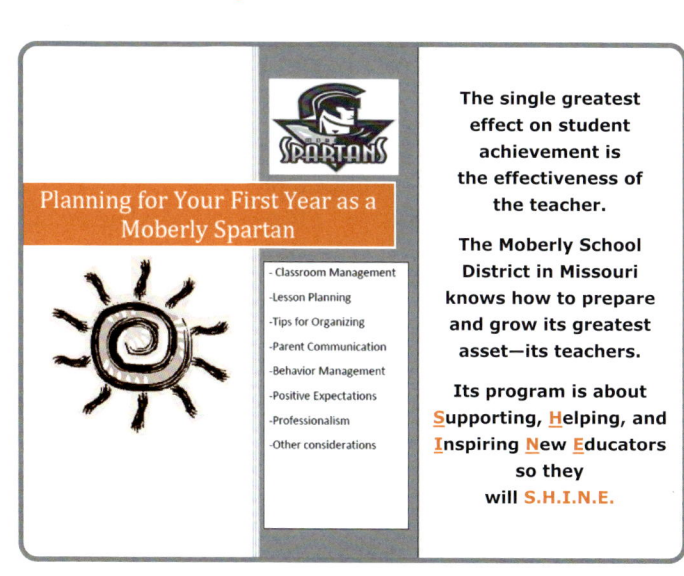

The Moberly induction program begins upon hiring. New teachers are contacted by the S.H.I.N.E. coordinator and welcomed to the district.

Chapter 5: Moberly School District • 41

Resources are shared for finding housing, learning about the community, as well as school-specific resources. Teachers are encouraged to come visit their school.

Each new teacher is paired with a retired teacher who provides positive encouragement and support. Isolation and working alone are not part of the Moberly culture. The emphasis is on team building to make a collaborative impact on new teachers and the students.

Two days of induction before school begins include classroom time with a collaborative tutor, technology training, elementary and secondary model classroom experiences, and learning district expectations.

A bus tour, formerly conducted by the leadership team, has been adopted by the Chamber of Commerce director who is the tour guide. The bus travels to each of the district's schools. At each school, the building principal/assistant principal "hops on the bus" and joins the teachers for the ride, sharing district information. Along the route, some of the community business sponsors place welcome signs, offer coupons, food or small gifts, and extend personal greetings. Stops include the local library, historic theater, and a clock tower/caboose that all connect to the history of Moberly.

Upon completion of a scavenger hunt, the group travels to the local park for a barbecue provided by two local businesses. Moberly Spartan shirts and business promotional items are given to the new teachers as welcoming gifts.

On the second day of orientation, the new teachers attend model classrooms for their grade level where they can see how classes are set up for the first days of school. Teachers study resource books on classroom management and effective instruction components.

Continuing with S.H.I.N.E.

A major component of the induction program is to teach and provide materials on how to plan and organize the classroom for student learning. Using *THE Classroom Management Book* as a reference, each teacher creates a classroom management plan in a binder, ready for the first days of school, and into which they continue to add during their career in Moberly.

Other components of the first year of the program provide whole group, one-on-one, and self-guided learning opportunities.

- There are six professional development workshops held throughout the school year—one full-day workshop, three after-school sessions, and two half-day workshops. During the day, workshops are held in off-campus locations to expose teachers to community resources and assets. Focus is on lesson planning, student learning, instruction, and classroom management.

- The teachers are taught how to utilize the district website including videos made by teachers with information on how to use district technology programs for taking attendance, entering grades, and logging parent communication. Common questions and anything that needs repeating from year to year is included on this website for teachers to return to whenever needed.

- A coach is provided to the new teacher from the same grade level or content area.

- There are weekly classroom visits and observations from the S.H.I.N.E. director and weekly reflection opportunities, including watching a video of themselves teaching.

- There is weekly collaboration in the professional learning community with cohorts in the same grade level/subject area.

- There are classroom release opportunities to observe other teachers.

- An end-of-year recognition celebration is held with the induction team, administrators, and school board members.

Year Two

Year Two teachers continue in the same cohort and work to further develop lesson planning, instruction, and classroom management strategies. They meet quarterly for professional development and continue to meet regularly with their coaches. They observe other classrooms, as well as participate in self-video reflection opportunities. They also have access to online professional development resources, organized social events, help from a retired teacher to provide positive encouragement, and updates and invitations to attend local events or activities in the community.

The Collaborative Impact

As the S.H.I.N.E program has been in existence for over ten years, new teacher support through both tutoring and coaching is now embedded in the culture of the Moberly School District. It is the expectation for the entire learning community to support one another. There is a common language, and all teachers model the foundations that have been developed with the beginning teachers. There is now an induction team of four as they have added a literacy coach, math coach, and an intervention/behavior coach to improve the training process.

The first- and second-year teachers learn that what Moberly does in its S.H.I.N.E. program is unmatched in surrounding districts, large or small.

The Moberly retention rate for beginning teachers is above 83 percent, which exceeds the state average of 60 percent over the past ten years.

As Moberly is a rural school district, teachers do sometimes leave for larger metropolitan districts near their homes or for family reasons. But when they leave, they are confident professionals, ready, willing, and able to tackle any challenges they may face elsewhere.

> **A trained teacher is always an asset wherever they are and wherever they go.**

Endnote

[1] "Teacher Attrition Costs United States Up to $2.2 Billion Annually, Says New Alliance Report," *Alliance for Excellent Education* (July 17, 2014).

Flowing Wells Unified School District

When teachers succeed, students succeed.

A Professional Development Center

The Flowing Wells Unified School District in Arizona has a dedicated professional development center with a small, full-time professional development staff.

The cornerstone of the district's training program is the Teacher Induction Program for Success (TIPS). The major goal of TIPS is to build a sense of culture and to articulate the district's mission and philosophy. The induction process is designed to train new teachers and teachers new to the district to the academic standards and vision of the district, and then continue the development of all teachers for the rest of their career, similar to the continuous professional development that is found in schools in all high-performing countries.

The Flowing Wells induction program is structured as a results-oriented staff development process. It emphasizes five critical attributes that are the cornerstones of its vision.

- Effective instructional practices
- Effective classroom management procedures and routines
- Awareness and understanding of the unique community they serve
- Teaching as lifelong learning with professional growth opportunities
- Teamwork among administrators, teachers, support staff, and community members

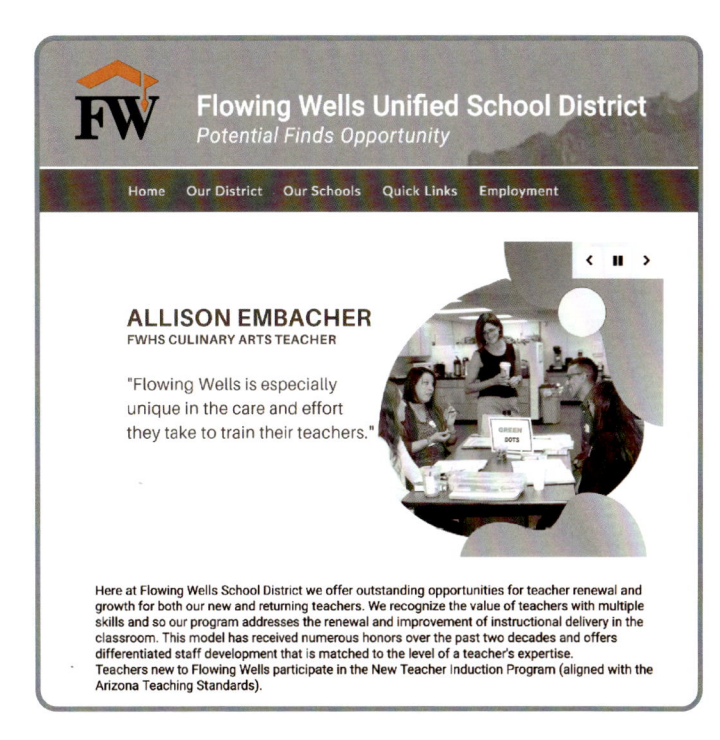

Flowing Wells Unified School District
Potential Finds Opportunity

Home   Our District   Our Schools   Quick Links   Employment

ALLISON EMBACHER
FWHS CULINARY ARTS TEACHER

"Flowing Wells is especially unique in the care and effort they take to train their teachers."

Here at Flowing Wells School District we offer outstanding opportunities for teacher renewal and growth for both our new and returning teachers. We recognize the value of teachers with multiple skills and so our program addresses the renewal and improvement of instructional delivery in the classroom. This model has received numerous honors over the past two decades and offers differentiated staff development that is matched to the level of a teacher's expertise. Teachers new to Flowing Wells participate in the New Teacher Induction Program (aligned with the Arizona Teaching Standards).

Chapter 6: Flowing Wells Unified School District • 45

35 YEARS OF DISTRICT SUPPORTED PROFESSIONAL DEVELOPMENT

- 6,000 HOURS OF CERTIFIED PD
- NATIONALLY RECOGNIZED INDUCTION PROGRAM
- STEMAZING TEACHER LEADERSHIP PROGRAM
- NATIONAL BOARD CANDIDATE SUPPORT
- 440 HOURS OF COACHING FOR TEACHERS

It all started in 1984 when the superintendent plucked an elementary teacher, **Susie Heintz**, and empowered her to create the district's staff development program—the **Institute for Teacher Renewal and Growth**.

The program is so successful in producing effective teachers that the Flowing Wells district has produced more teacher-of-the-year nominees and winners than any other district in the state of Arizona. They do this by taking novice teachers and turning them into expert teachers with a multiyear, new teacher induction and lifelong professional development program. The district excels in building human capacity.

The Flowing Wells professional development program is the key element for its many successes. The results achieved through the years are remarkable and validate the strength of the process.

- Seven Arizona Teacher-of-the-Year awards
- Sixteen Arizona Top 5 Teacher-of-the-Year awards
- Seventeen Top 10 Teacher-of-the-Year awards
- Two Milken National Educator Awards
- One National Teacher-of-the-Year finalist
- One National Assistant Principal-of-the-Year award
- Four Arizona Superintendent-of-the-Year awards from Arizona School Administrators and/or American Association of School Administrators
- All eight traditional schools have received the Arizona Education Association's "A+" award. (The alternative high school is not eligible for this award.)
- Seven of eight traditional schools have received the U.S. Department of Education's "National Blue Ribbon Schools" award.
- Flowing Wells High School was ranked by the *U.S. News & World Report* as a Silver Award Winner in its "2012 Best Schools in America" report.
- At Flowing Wells High School (total 1,623 students) enrollment in Honors and AP courses for the 2021–2022 school year was 553 students enrolled out of a total of 902 Honors/AP sections (some students have multiple advanced courses).
- Two teachers have won the Presidential Award for Excellence in Mathematics and Science Teaching.
- Twenty teachers have earned National Board Certification.

TEACHER INDUCTION

Congratulations 2019-2020 Induction Graduates!!

Flowing Wells has a commitment to unleashing the potential in its teachers.

Implementing the Induction Program

The district's Teacher Induction Program for Success (TIPS) includes
- an eight-day induction program beginning with four days before school begins, and
- four days during the school year (release time for new teachers).

Preschool Orientation: TIPS starts with four days of intensive training in early August before the school year begins. Participation is mandatory for first-time teachers, and extra days are added to their contracts so that they can participate in induction. On the morning of **Day 1**, new teachers are greeted by the induction team, the superintendent, and members of the supervisory staff. The feelings of teamwork and collegial support are immediately evident as the new team members are welcomed aboard. Refreshments are served, pictures are taken, new teachers are organized into cooperative groups, and the instruction begins. The setting is that of a model classroom, with the induction team representing the teachers and the new teachers representing the students. The teachers are given
- a letter of welcome from the superintendent,
- a copy of the district's mission and goals,
- information on each of the schools in Flowing Wells,
- information on what to expect from induction and what it looks like throughout the first year of teaching and beyond,
- information on the Flowing Wells ongoing career development program,
- classroom management tips,
- a glossary of education terms, and
- a sample first-day checklist.

The first three days of induction are devoted to effective instructional practices. This is logical because the research on instruction is overwhelming.

> **It is teachers and their instructional practices, not programs or changes to school structure, that improve student learning.**

Day 2 continues with instruction on the elements of effective instruction where teachers, in their cooperative groups, create instructional objectives and plan sample lessons.

On **Day 3**, along with more instruction on effective instruction, there is information on health care insurance, the culture of the Flowing Wells Unified School District, and the unique needs of the population.

They view a video titled "The Flowing Wells Community in Action." Then, new teachers board a school bus with the superintendent for a guided tour of the Flowing Wells community. A special luncheon is sponsored by the Flowing Wells Education Association.

In the afternoon new teachers report to their respective schools for planning time with the principals, where curriculum and school procedures are discussed.

Day 4 is focused on classroom management. The new teachers are asked to read the chapters in *THE First Days of School* on classroom management, and then they are taken to visit demonstration classrooms to observe how master teachers organize and prepare the procedures needed on their first day.

Classroom visits are organized in advance by hiring four or five master teachers (from various grade levels and content areas) to get their rooms ready early and to host a group of new teachers for approximately two hours.

New teachers see the importance of bellwork, procedures, and routines in a classroom setting. They also learn to formulate a discipline plan

Chapter 6: Flowing Wells Unified School District • 47

Welcome, New Teachers, to Demo Classroom:

The First Day

with clearly stated rules and consequences. New teachers are encouraged to photograph the organization and procedures posted in the classrooms of master teachers to use a model as they create the environment for their classroom.

The master teachers demonstrate their simulated first day of school with the new teachers as their "students." The master teachers then debrief the simulation with the new teachers (these could be veteran teachers who are new to Flowing Wells), helping them to analyze the many procedures and management strategies that are woven into the simulation. This is especially powerful because it also helps the new teachers see how to organize and plan the first days of school.

The master teachers provide the new teachers with print or electronic copies of everything demonstrated during the simulation. After a debriefing of their visit to the demonstration classroom, they then implement the organizational procedures for their own first day of school.

> *After induction I went to the classroom, started with a few procedures, and then went right into teaching English, which is what I had been waiting to do.*
>
> Toby Gregory

The First Years Continued

Four additional days during the school year are devoted to professional development. This same continuous professional development is offered for the rest of a teacher's career.

During the entire year, the staff development administrator serves as a coach to all new teachers, visiting each at least five times. The purpose of these observations is to help new teachers strengthen their skills and address any weaknesses. Also, each school site has a volunteer coordinator who meets bimonthly with new teachers to offer support.

Sometime in late March or early April, the new teachers are honored with a graduation celebration in a beautifully decorated boardroom. Induction graduates sit with their principals and district administrators and enjoy a formal, candlelit luncheon. The superintendent presents framed certificates to the graduates.

<u>Year Two</u>: During the teachers' second year, instructional coordinators continue their work with them. These coordinators are teachers who receive stipends and release time to work with the teachers they are training. Instructional strategies, professional classroom management techniques, parent techniques, and policies and procedures receive continued emphasis.

<u>Years Three and Four</u>: In the third and fourth years, teachers receive advanced training in instructional strategies, cooperative learning, higher-level thinking, and more. Instructional coordinators continue to observe and support these teachers.

Flowing Wells has a plan to engage new teachers in a systemic onboarding process that is carried out over days, weeks, months, and years of a teacher's professional journey.

Continuous Professional Development

In Flowing Wells it is difficult to determine where one aspect of professional development ends and another begins—the transition is that smooth. Professional development is ongoing and career long, with training that is very specific to the stages of teacher growth. Therefore, induction has no clear-cut timelines. New teachers are inducted during their initial years and the training and support simply meld into ongoing, career-long professional development.

The process of continuous professional development is similar to what happens in all the high-performing countries. This is the way induction should proceed, and it is one of the main reasons that Flowing Wells is one of the most effective school districts in the United States.

From Novice to Expert Teachers

The district's professional development program takes a teacher through five incremental stages, from "novice" (first-year teachers), to "advanced beginner" (second-year teachers), to "competent" (third-year teachers), and then to "proficient" and "expert" (ensuing years). This then flows seamlessly into a lifelong professional development program called the Institute for Teacher Renewal and Growth. **Flowing Wells's mission is unmistakable—to produce effective teachers who can teach.**

At each level there is structured training, along with formative and summative observations and evaluations. In Flowing Wells there's something for everyone at all levels of teaching and professional growth.

Formalized Training Chart

Flowing Wells has a formalized, professional new teacher induction program that is

- **comprehensive** in its offerings for teacher development,
- **coherent** with articulated goals and vision, and
- **continuous** in its efforts to create expert teachers and to keep them in the district.

The Outcomes

The Flowing Wells induction program is effective.

- One hundred percent of all new teachers to Flowing Wells attend the induction program during their first full year in the district.

- Approximately 70 percent of all Flowing Wells teachers attend staff development training each year on a voluntary basis.

- Based on feedback from school principals, the quality of teaching performance has improved significantly.

Flowing Wells Unified School District
New Teacher Induction – Formal Training
"New Teacher" includes all teachers new to Flowing Wells

	NEW TEACHERS Total # of hours	INDUCTION DAYS 1–4 # of hours	ONGOING TRAINING # of hours
Organizational Culture: Giving information to transmit the culture of the system and organization with guidelines, expectations, policies, procedures, customs, beliefs, and core values	4 hours	3 hours	1 hour
Systems Information: Giving information related to procedures, guidelines, and expectations of the school district and the school	4 hours	3 hours	1 hour Ongoing through mentorship and "New Teacher Meetings"
Resources: Collecting, disseminating, or locating materials or other resources	1 hour		1 hour Ongoing through mentorship and "New Teacher Meetings"
Instructional Information: Giving information about teaching strategies or the instructional process	28 hours	11 hours	17 hours
Emotional Support: Offering support by listening empathetically and sharing experiences	3 hours	1 hour	2 hours and Ongoing at follow-up coaching and "New Teacher Meetings"
Advice on Student Management: Giving guidance and ideas related to discipline and managing students *All new teachers receive an advance copy of THE First Days of School by Harry and Rosemary Wong.	2 hours	2 hours	Ongoing at follow-up sessions and "New Teacher Meetings"
Advice on Scheduling and Planning: Offering information about organizing and planning the school day	1 hour		1 hour Ongoing through mentorship and "New Teacher Meetings"
Help with Classroom Environment: Helping arrange, organize, or analyze the physical setting of the classroom	2 hours	2 hours	Ongoing through mentorship and "New Teacher Meetings"
Demonstration Teaching: Teaching while new teacher observes, preceded and followed with conferencing to focus and analyze instructional strategies	7 hours	2 hours	5 hours
Coaching: Critiquing and providing feedback on the teacher's performance	10 hours		10 hours
Advice on Working with Parents: Giving help or ideas related to conferencing or working with parents			Ongoing through mentorship and "New Teacher Meetings"
Special Education Issues:	1 hour		1 hour Ongoing through mentorship and "New Teacher Meetings"
Other topics or activities: See Professional Development brochure for ongoing professional development program for second-year teachers and above. • New teacher contract includes four before school induction days—no extra money. • Substitutes are hired for teachers who attend workshops during school hours. • Methods used to evaluate success: — Participant feedback — Teacher retention — Teachers' voluntary participation in workshops beginning in 2nd year — Recruitment numbers — Student test scores used to provide areas for professional development focus			

- "Proficient" and "expert" teachers act as instructional coaches who provide continued new teacher support at individual sites.

- An increased ability for teachers to reflect on their instructional practices has promoted professional dialogue among teachers, support staff, and community.

- An attitude that professional growth is the norm for a Flowing Wells educator is evidenced by participation in after school and summer workshops.

What Keeps Effective Teachers

Teaching in seclusion is not justifiable. **Good teaching thrives in sustained teacher networks in a collaborative learning environment created by teachers and school leaders working together to improve learning and collaboration in strong, professional communities.**

> **Collaboration is the most effective way for teachers to learn.**

Effective school districts successfully train and nurture all teachers to reach great heights. Every moment of each day is an opportunity for teachers to grow and learn and reach the top of their profession. Students learn from how well teachers teach. Students do not learn from programs, technology, or ideologies. The emphasis of the Flowing Wells professional learning program is on effective instructional practices.

Effective school districts use induction programs and comprehensive professional development to build teacher capacity.

It is the improved capacity of teachers that instructs students. As the cadre of teachers becomes more and more effective, students will learn more and more and achieve higher and higher results.

When teachers succeed, students succeed.

For almost forty years, Flowing Wells has been improving the instructional practices of its teachers and creating effective schools. Flowing Wells has clearly demonstrated that professional development produces astounding results for teachers and for students.

7 The Stay Interview

A stay interview is a dialogue, a conversation, not an evaluation of a teacher's performance.

Not Your Typical Interview

A stay interview is a structured discussion conducted with an individual teacher to strengthen the teacher's engagement and retention. It is the opposite of an exit interview. The time is spent reviewing teacher responsibilities, assisting in realizing personal goals, and enjoying being part of the team.

> A stay interview is a "happiness check-in."

A stay interview is a positive interaction that promotes an inclusive and caring culture.

Effectiveness of Stay Interviews

Using this technique, 94 percent of teachers in five districts in Maricopa County, Arizona, were retained in the 2020–21 school year. These Title I schools generally had a 50 percent higher attrition rate than higher-income, non-Title I schools.

The **Phoenix Elementary School District** was one of the systems that retained its teachers at a higher rate. Implementing the stay interview process, they saw "teacher retention over 90 percent," said **Victor Diaz**, Director of Human Resources in the district. "Elsewhere in Arizona, attrition rates were 20 to 30 percent."[1]

What's remarkable about the stay interview process and its effectiveness is that the teachers who were exposed to the method are the district's rock stars. They are irreplaceable. They are like the all-stars on a team. They drive the success of the team. They drive the success of the school. They drive the success of the district.

Why Have a Stay Interview?

Conducting these interviews sends a very strong message to your teachers that their voice matters, and they have the opportunity to share any concerns as well as their appreciation for what is working well.

These check-ins can be particularly valuable with high-performing employees to connect with them well before they may seriously consider leaving.

Instead of asking why a teacher is exiting, **a stay interview focuses on what motivates the teacher to continue staying at the school**, what could be better about their teaching experience, and how they envision the next stage of their career within the profession.

View the stay interview as a conversation, not as an interview. Approach the time together as one to establish deeper connection with these discussion starters.

- Help me understand how you're doing.
- Share with me your goals.
- Tell me what we can do this year to make sure you're thriving and staying enthusiastic about your career.
- Tell me what we can do for you next school year to keep you excited about teaching.

Organization of Stay Interviews

A stay interview takes place during the school year, not at year's end, and it's conducted primarily with employees that you don't want to lose—rather than those who won't be returning the next school year. An ideal time to conduct the interview is a month or two after the start of the new school year so teachers have had some time to settle into the routine of the year, but before they have any thoughts of leaving.

An investment of time shows a school's commitment to growing and developing quality teachers.

Stay interviews are organized to make positive change to retain employees. The best stay interview helps your most valuable teachers understand their importance and your commitment to their success.

- You recognize and appreciate their loyalty.
- You care about more than just their classroom performance.
- You're open to making changes that would bring them more satisfaction and greater professional success.

Stay interviews are informal conversations. Stay interviews build trust as this will improve engagement and retention and build a more productive one-on-one relationship.

> **Teachers will only share how they feel about work honestly if they feel a sense of mental safety without fear of retaliation.**

Focus on how teachers feel about the work they do every day, the value of their contributions, and how they feel within the organization. This is not a time to share status updates about projects that need to be done.

Most important, this is not time to talk about a teacher's performance. This is a discussion—a conversation—not an evaluation. It's a time of reflection and envisioning the future.

Clearly separate stay interviews from performance reviews. Ironically, your teachers are really evaluating the performance of **you** during this beneficial one-on-one time together.

Chapter 7: The Stay Interview • 53

> *Without reflection, we go blindly on our way, creating more unintended consequences, and failing to achieve anything useful.*
>
> — Margaret J. Wheatley

Preparation for a Stay Interview

Clarify the purpose of the meeting.
Be transparent about what a stay interview is and that you are conducting it to gain a better understanding of what is best for teacher happiness and student success. Stay interviews should focus on how the teacher feels about the work they do every day, the value of their contributions, and how they feel within the organization. **This is a discussion about a teacher's professional journey.** It is not a time to share updates on outstanding work, issues, or problem students.

Give teachers time to prepare.
No one likes to be blindsided, so it's important that you give your teachers ample time to prepare for a stay interview. Ideally, provide four or five questions beforehand that will serve as a guide to the upcoming conversation.

Pick a comfortable setting for the teacher.
A stay interview should feel like a coffee house chat, not an interrogation. The stay interview is an ideal way to make teachers feel they matter. Teachers want to be seen, heard, and valued, so genuinely act on their feedback, otherwise it means nothing to the teacher and similar attempts in the future will fail.

Time the stay interviews soon after the start of the school year.
Conducting the stay interview soon after the start of the school year allows plenty of time to address concerns raised during these conversations. Even though the interview is structured with your questions, keep the conversation to about thirty minutes, but it can be repeated two to three times each year. The brief conversations have considerable benefit as they provide key insights into what factors are encouraging your teachers to stay and the issues that might be prompting them to consider leaving.

What to Ask During a Stay Interview

Listen 80 percent of the time. Enter the meeting with a commitment to ask, listen, and only ask again once you've digested all you've heard. You can demonstrate this by taking notes. Probe to learn more. Probing shows you care.

Taking notes depicts you as an active listener.

Make teachers feel like they matter and that they belong because of your stay interview with them. Ask what they think and genuinely get to know their thoughts. Send the teacher a few starter questions to prepare for the conversation ahead of time.

- What excites you about coming to work each day?
- Do you feel good about the impact of your work?
- What do you want to do more of at work? Less?
- Do you see a future for yourself at this school or district?
- If you were principal for a day, how would you spend your time?

Monitor the stay interview time ensuring it is a two-way dialogue rather than an interview. Ask for teacher feedback and assure the teacher that the feedback will be fully accepted. This includes asking what could be improved or better at the school and what are some areas where you as a principal or administrator can improve. If such questions are asked, it is important you share your own perspective as well as part of the dialogue.

Ending a Stay Interview

Follow a few simple steps to close a stay interview. Thank the teacher for taking the time to meet with you, summarize the feedback you've heard, relay what your next steps will be, and provide a clear sense of what the teacher can expect will be different following the conversation.

Why Have a Stay Interview?

> While seemingly this process is time consuming, know that it takes a lot more time to recruit and hire an untrained teacher than it does to retain one.

Principals like to say that they have an open-door policy, but do little to encourage it or define exactly what that means in a meaningful and consistent manner. Other principals may wait until an exit interview—at which point it's likely too late to do anything meaningful to convince a teacher to stay at the school.

Having a teacher for more than one year leads to a greater likelihood of student academic achievement and attendance. A **Rockefeller Institute of Government** report concluded that the student-teacher relationship is particularly important in determining the student's success. In fact, students who have the same teacher more than once showed greater levels of achievement and fewer absences, truancies, and suspensions.

A student knows what to expect in terms of classroom procedures and structure. They already have experience in the way a teacher assigns homework or other assignments. And they may experience less stress at the beginning of the year worrying about the unknown if they already know the teacher.

High-achieving students and white female students see larger increases in test scores in math and English with repeat teachers when compared to their peers. In addition, students whose test scores are lower, as well as male students of color, see fewer absences and suspensions when compared to their peers.[2]

Matthew Kraft from Brown University says, "You can just imagine being a student in a class where most of your peers have had that teacher before. Our evidence demonstrates that students who have had a teacher before are likely to perform better academically. They also show up more to class and are less likely to be suspended."[3]

In essence, **a stay interview is a powerful indicator of your skill as a leader.** This is when your teachers can see that you are a great educator. During the conversation, teachers will see that you are patient and caring, tolerant of mistakes, but mostly encouraging in their growth as a professional educator.

The goal of a stay interview is to keep your valuable teachers as they are the ones who will be the celebrated assets for your school. They will be the ones responsible for the achievement gains realized by your students.

Teachers are a school's most valuable asset. Create a sense of belonging with the stay interview to make your teachers feel their worth.

Checklist for Induction Leaders and Principals

- ☐ Schedule new teacher orientation in addition to regular teacher orientation. (New teachers attend both sessions.)
- ☐ Assign new teachers a fair mix of classes, students, and facility resources. (If possible, lighten their load for the first year.)
- ☐ Assign a duty schedule with moderate difficulty and requiring moderate amounts of time so it's not too demanding for the new teacher.
- ☐ Appoint someone to help new teachers set up their classrooms.
- ☐ Pair new teachers with master teachers to meet regularly to identify general problems before they become serious.
- ☐ Provide coaching groups, tutor groups, or collaborative problem-solving groups for all new teachers to attend.
- ☐ Provide time for observations, joint planning, team teaching, committee assignments, and other cooperative arrangements between new and experienced teachers.
- ☐ Schedule individual stay interviews within the first two months of school.
- ☐ Schedule informal, reinforcing events, involving new and experienced teachers, such as luncheons, socials, and awards.
- ☐ Plan special and continuing in-service activities with topics directly related to the needs and interests of new teachers. (Eventually, integrate new professional development activities with regular professional development activities and training.)
- ☐ Issue newsletters to parents and to the community that report on accomplishments of all teachers, especially new teachers.
- ☐ Perform regular assessment of new teachers; evaluate strengths and weaknesses, present new information, demonstrate new skills, and provide opportunities for practice and feedback.
- ☐ Celebrate successful first year of teaching with new teachers.

Endnotes

[1] Elizabeth Heubeck, "The Stay Interview: How It Can Help Schools Hold Onto Valued Staff," *Education Week* (June 22, 2022).

[2] Leigh Wedenoja, "Teacher Looping Improves Student Outcomes," (Rockefeller Institute of Government, November 21, 2019) https://rockinst.org/blog/teacher-looping-improves-student-outcomes/.

[3] Micah Ward, "Repeat Teachers: The Benefits of Sustained Student-Teacher Relationships," *District Administrator* (July 1, 2022).

High-Performing Induction Programs

8 **High-Performing School Systems**
High-performing school systems empower their teachers with continuous professional development. **59**

9 **High-Performing Companies**
New employees are trained immediately so that they can successfully accomplish the requirements of their job. **72**

10 **Return on Investment**
The greatest tragedy is the annual loss from not harnessing the potential intellectual capacity of new teachers. **77**

High-Performing School Systems

High-performing school systems empower their teachers with continuous professional development.

Building Capacity

There is one defining indicator of every high-performing school system. It is an **unwavering focus on training and supporting teachers, from their preservice work until retirement.** Building capacity requires a shared commitment between teachers and administrators.

> The high-performing countries of the world develop, sustain, and retain their most effective teachers.

Beginning with a new teacher induction program, high-performing countries build the capacity of their teacher workforce. To build teacher capacity is to focus on and develop the aptitudes and skills teachers need to become adept classroom managers and effective instructors who make an impact on their students.

Every business owner strives to build capacity to be successful and improve profits. Farmers must contend with reduced soil fertility, erratic weather, and changing markets. To build and maximize capacity, they use their agricultural knowledge and basic business skills to generate more productivity and income. People in the entertainment and sports industries delight in performing at full capacity—both personally and in packed stadiums and theaters.

High-performing school systems throughout the world constantly build the capacity of their teachers to be more and more effective in teaching students a content-rich curriculum.

Failure to Build Capacity

Regretfully, building the capacity for educators to excel in teaching the curriculum is virtually unknown in the United States. Instead, school systems rely on makeshift fads of the moment, buying more and more technology, asking for smaller class sizes, and more counselors and social workers. Inconclusive debates on personalized versus whole class instruction, phonics versus whole language, and so on are never-ending.

> In the United States, we think we can buy our way into student achievement. There is almost never a discussion about building teacher capacity.

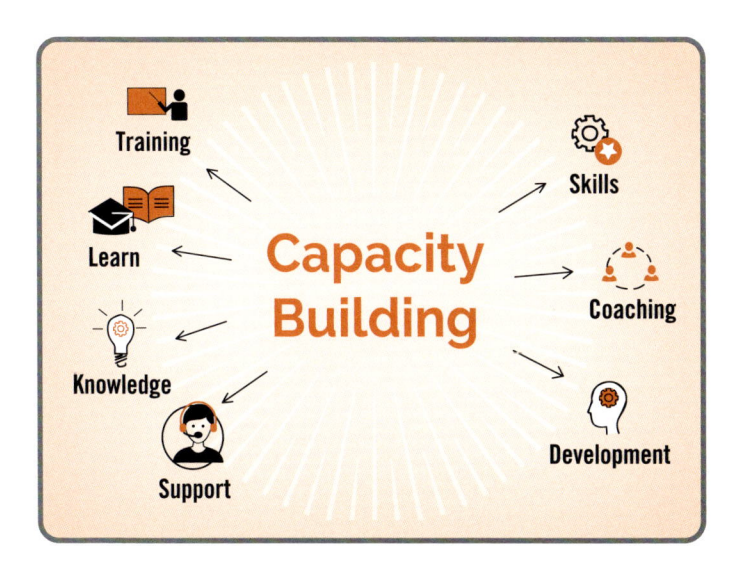

Chapter 8: High-Performing School Systems • 59

We Hire Teachers After the School Year Has Started

In high-performing countries, teachers are "hired" when they are in high school. That is, their system pursues high-achieving students and encourages them to become teachers. They then matriculate as a cohort, getting to know each other and collaborating as they proceed through a school of education.

Research from the **Harvard Graduate School of Education** reveals that many schools in the United States are not organized to hire and support new teachers in ways that help them transition into the profession smoothly and attain early success.

- Thirty-three percent of new teachers are hired after the school year has already started, and 62 percent are hired within thirty days of when they start teaching.
- Only 50 percent of new teachers interview with any of their future teacher colleagues as part of the hiring process.
- There is no induction process available to 56 percent of new teachers to help them learn.

We not only hire teachers after the school year has started, but all too often teachers are just thrown into the classroom to survive.

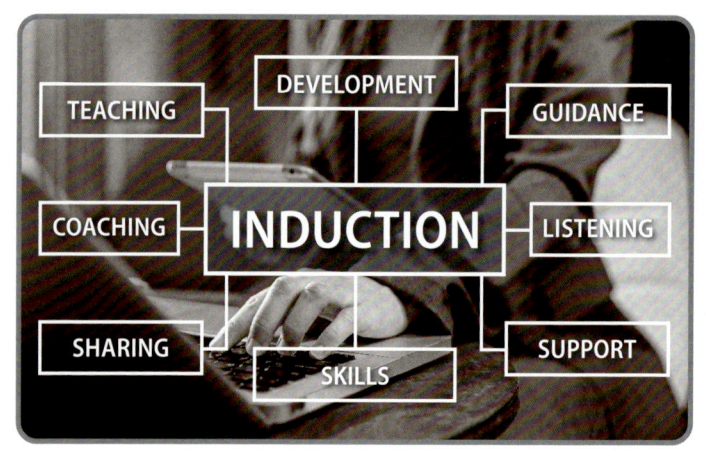

Capacity is built with a variety of methods embedded in an induction program.

Why Schools Succeed

To understand why some schools succeed where others do not, **McKinsey & Company**, *Insights on Education*, reported on studies of twenty-five of the world's school systems, including ten of the top performers.[1] The experience of these top school systems indicates that these three things matter most.

1. Getting the right people to become teachers
2. Developing teachers into effective instructors
3. Ensuring the system is available to deliver the best possible instruction for every student

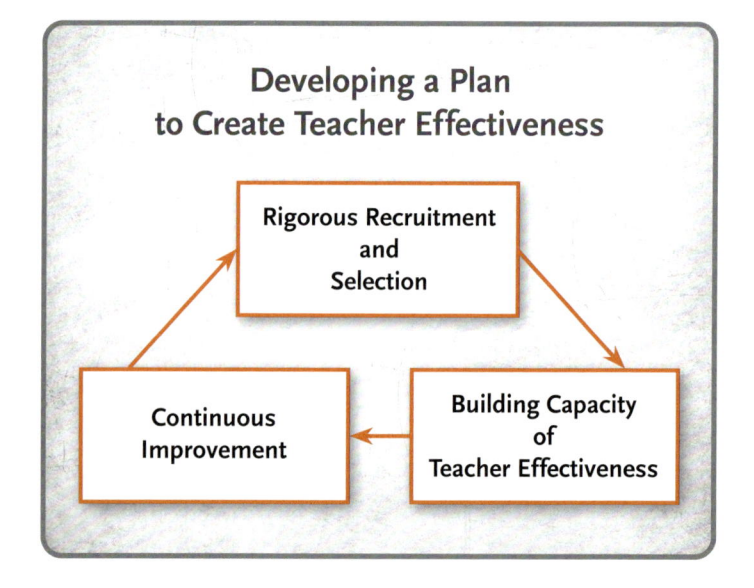

Developing a Plan to Create Teacher Effectiveness

Rigorous Recruitment and Selection → Building Capacity of Teacher Effectiveness → Continuous Improvement → (back to Rigorous Recruitment and Selection)

Induction in Finland

Helsinki University

Pauli Virtanen breathed a sigh of relief when he was notified that he had been accepted into one of the eleven universities devoted exclusively to the training and preparation of teachers in Finland. Of those who applied to be primary school teachers, he was one of the 6.7 percent accepted. That's a lower acceptance rate than the 10 percent of applicants admitted to the University of Helsinki's schools of law and medicine. While at the university, Pauli must acquire a master's degree and complete the equivalent of a residency program like in medical schools.

Annual national opinion polls have repeatedly shown that teaching is one of Finland's most admired professions, and primary school teaching is the most sought-after career. Teachers are regarded as the key for the future, and they are recruited from the top quartile of the college-bound cohort. Once an applicant makes it beyond this first screening round, they are then observed in a teaching-like activity and interviewed. Only candidates with a clear aptitude for teaching in addition to strong academic performance are admitted to a school of education.

There are eleven universities specifically designated as teacher training schools scattered around the country in Finland. Teacher education is strongly research-based with an emphasis on pedagogical content knowledge. Teachers are didacticians—they can connect teaching effectiveness with sound evidence. They must spend a full year teaching in a teacher training school where prospective teachers and researchers develop and model new practices and complete research on teaching and learning. **They enter the teaching profession knowing what to do.**

Finland holds its educators in highest esteem.

From the minute they begin teaching, they learn how to participate in problem-solving groups to create effective lessons and to improve their teaching skills, performance, and outcomes. Involvement in these meetings is structured into part of a Finnish teacher's workload.

No one teaches in isolation in Finland. Groups of teachers visit each other's classrooms and plan lessons together in a system that includes "rounds" similar to those in the medical profession. Just as you trust your doctor, the people of Finland trust their teachers. Teachers share their students' progress with other teachers as they make their rounds.

Finland is one of the most northern countries in the world. With a population of more than 5.5 million, its post-secondary education is ranked number one in the world by the **World Economic Forum**—and education is free for its citizens.

The culture in Finland is that you are part of professional networks, sharing ideas and best practices.

In Finland, education practices come with no political baggage. **The government makes its education policy decisions based almost solely on effectiveness.** If the data show improvements, the Ministry of Education and Culture will encourage teachers to implement its usage. Finland invests in building a high-capacity teaching workforce and the result is that Finland has one of the smallest learning gaps between low-income and high-income young people. Finland's educational policies are largely in the hands of trusted experts— the educators—and the country is now a world leader in education. Teachers in Finland are autonomous professionals respected for making a difference in young people's lives.

Finland has a very high retention rate for teachers. Over 90 percent of trained teachers remain in the profession for the duration of their careers.

Induction in Singapore

Ayesha Gill lives in Singapore. She was in the upper third of her high school class so she was recruited to become a teacher.

Teaching is a highly respected profession in Singapore because everyone knows how hard it is to be accepted into the **National Institute of Education (NIE)**, the only institute of education. The many steps in the application process include tough panel interviews that focus on the personal qualities that make for a good teacher, as well as intensive reviews of academic records and contributions applicants have made to their respective schools and communities.

To become a teacher, one must master the subject one is going to teach at a high level, as well as have at least a year of challenging instruction in the craft of teaching.

If you ever have the opportunity to visit a school in Singapore, you will constantly hear the teachers refer to each other as "colleagues." **The prevailing**

Colleagues working and planning together is commonplace among Singapore's teachers.

culture is that collaborative sharing is ubiquitous and consistent in Singapore.

New teachers will find the entire staff is there to support and help them learn to be successful. Everyone aspires to help them adjust, improve, and perform. The minute they start, they have an assigned senior teacher-coach. In addition, they will also have a buddy-coach in the same subject or in the same department to navigate the ins and outs of teaching. New teachers are observed and tutored by grade-level chairs, subject-area chairs, and department heads. The system is rigorous, and poor attitude and lack of professionalism or improvement are not tolerated.

The teachers of Singapore have formed their own organization, the **Academy of Singapore Teachers**, to define their profession. They created an explicit model, the **Singapore Teaching Practice**, outlining how effective teaching and learning is achieved in their schools. It provides a shared language and commonly understood set of references, visions, and experiences which teachers can use to collaborate.

The Singapore Teaching Practice has defined areas.

- Understanding Students and Learning
- Understanding Subject Matter and Goals
- Understanding Teaching
- Pedagogical Practices
- Singapore Curriculum and Philosophy

These practices and dedication highlight that teaching in Singapore is practiced as a profession whereas, in the United States, education is essentially an occupation without a professional practice or culture. **There is no common teaching model in the United States educational system.**

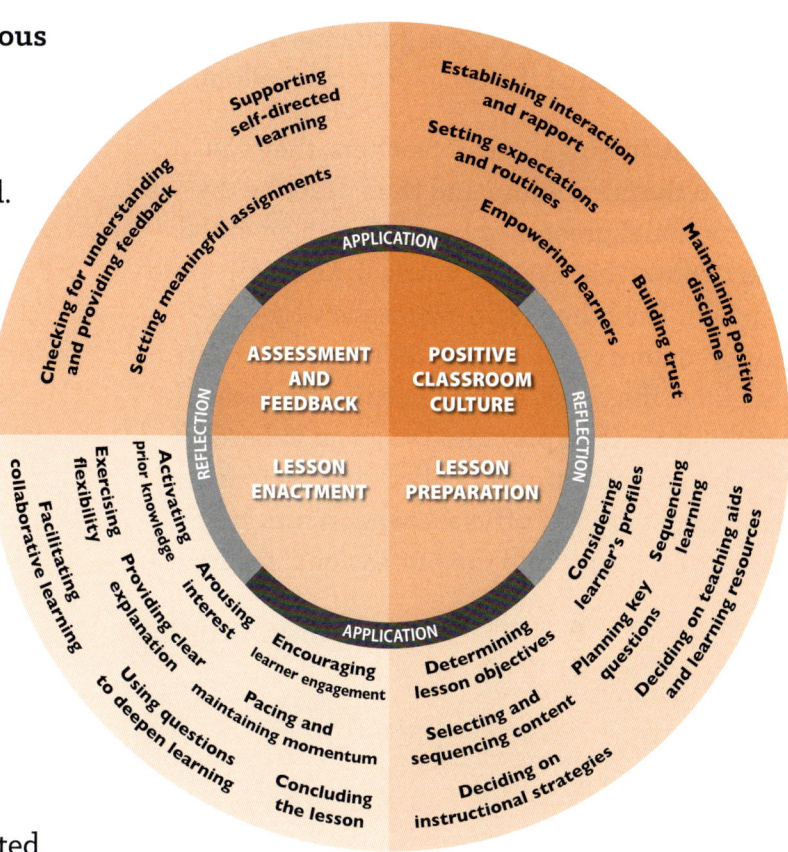

The four teaching processes specify the actions needed to facilitate learning in students ensuring consistency in teaching practices.

The Singapore Teaching Practice ensures that professional development takes place in a targeted manner. Professional development is curriculum-specific and deals concretely with what is to be taught in the classroom, not with whatever the current fad is or grant that was obtained.

> The Singapore Teaching Practice Model produces teachers with such effective potential that the Singapore school system is, arguably, the best school system in the world.

The Singapore Teaching Practice presents educators with core beliefs that drive their teaching and learning. These beliefs, which place every student

Chapter 8: High-Performing School Systems • 63

at the heart of their choices, guide the design and implementation of the Singapore curriculum.

If you talk to Singaporean teachers, they can explain the curriculum and then describe the instructional process of how it is implemented. They know what aspects to use to be an effective teacher. They then train themselves for one hundred hours each year until they retire. During this time, the teachers who become proficient in teaching are then promoted to go on to become coaches, administrators, college instructors, and education ministry officials, who in turn help their colleagues climb the professional ladder.

The excellence of education in Singapore has all happened in a few decades (Singapore was founded in 1965) because the government made it a mission to build the capacity of their citizens through education.

There are three directions a teaching career can take in Singapore.

1. Teaching track
2. Leadership track
3. Specialist track

Depending on performance and potential, a teacher who opts to be in the **teaching track** will move from being a senior teacher to becoming a principal master teacher whose responsibilities include coaching and pedagogical leadership.

For the **leadership track**, the teacher moves from subject head or head of department to principalship or other leadership roles in the ministry.

Teachers on the **specialist track** move from senior specialist to becoming a principal specialist.

All teachers are observed for three years to determine which career path would best suit them. Talent and potential for leadership are identified early, and these teachers are then groomed for future leadership roles.

Singaporean schools operate under the belief that poor leadership is a major reason for school failure and by choosing talented individuals early in their careers and investing in them heavily, schools can avoid this problem. This training often involves promotion to department head at a young age, recruitment to several academic and administrative committees, stints at the Ministry of Education, and a six-month executive leadership course at the National Institute of Education (NIE).

Instruction at the NIE and policy determination at the Ministry of Education is based on building the capacity of its teachers and then empowering them to do the work of improving the system to create, develop, and assess for student learning.

Teachers are proud of a system that seamlessly connects the preservice training experienced at the National Institute of Education and ongoing professional development at the school level. The system pays just as much attention to how teachers develop their identity as professionals as to their pedagogical content knowledge.

Singaporean administrators know education. They know instruction. To become a principal, they must know how to teach and can train neophyte teachers in how to teach. Before becoming an administrator, they must pass through and demonstrate that they are effective teachers. Then they take extensive leadership and curriculum classes before they are entrusted with producing effective teachers, like themselves.

In high-performing school systems, principals are promoted from within the profession after they have shown that they are superior, effective teachers.

The quality of Singapore school principals is directly related to the
- high standards that applicants must meet to become a teacher, and
- the fact that the only avenue to becoming a principal comes from promotion up the career ladder.

Once they become teachers, only three to four percent of teachers in Singapore leave the profession each year, usually for retirement. In the United States, annual teacher attrition is about 8 percent and accounts for roughly 90 percent of the demand for new teachers.[2] **It is extremely rare to have new teacher attrition in Singapore or in Finland.**

Induction in Japan

Shota Matsumoto, as a first-year teacher in Tokyo, was immediately immersed in the culture of collaboration at his school. On the first moment of his first day as a teacher, he was escorted to the common office that all teachers at his school share and was introduced to all his colleagues. This is a large room where each teacher has a desk and is surrounded by all the materials, technology, and equipment needed to prepare lessons. Periodicals and reference materials abound. There are coffee and tea pots and sofas for relaxing and chatting.

Working together and respecting colleagues are elements that onboard new teachers quickly in high-performing school systems.

Because everyone knows what to do, they will teach Shota what to do. New teachers are tutored by their colleagues and administrators, the people with whom they will be working. Veteran teachers want new teachers to be up-to-speed as quickly as possible because they are all part of a team.

All teachers in Japan are part of an instructional process where cooperative groups of veteran and junior teachers are immersed in "lesson study" in which groups of teachers review their lessons and consider how to improve them. As the name implies, the group designs and perfects lessons that make an impact on student learning.

Shota Matsumoto (upper right) and his colleagues work collaboratively on perfecting the instruction they are going to deliver to students.

Lesson study is a simple idea. If you want to improve instruction, what could be more obvious than collaborating with fellow teachers to plan, observe, and reflect on lessons? During lesson study, teachers research and design a lesson, and then present it to other teachers, who give feedback. It's not about an individual teacher, but about teamwork.

In Japan, all new teachers typically teach two or more demonstration lessons during their first year that are viewed by prefectural administrators, the guiding teacher, the school principal/assistant principal, and other teachers in the school.

Teachers in Japan are hired not by individual schools, but by prefectures, which are roughly analogous to states. Their school assignments within the prefecture change every three years or so in the beginning of their careers, and then not quite as often later in their careers. This means that the prefectural government can make sure the strongest teachers are assigned to the students and schools that need them the most. Young teachers are exposed to different environments and to a series of various talented peers so that they learn from their methods.

"Cleanliness is a mindset—a positive habit that keeps the body, mind, and environment happy, healthy, simple, neat, and delightful."—Amit Ray

In addition to academic instruction, schools also seek to teach morals to their students to raise well rounded, thoughtful human beings. Students are responsible for keeping their school clean and well-maintained. It is simply part of their daily routine.[3]

Induction in Canada

In just over a decade, the Canadian province of Ontario has dramatically improved its education system to become one of the best in the world. How the sprawling province has done this can be contained in two simple words, "capacity building." **Building capacity means developing all teachers so they know what to do to improve student learning and achievement.**

As recently as 2002, Ontario was in political turmoil with much bickering and the school system was stagnant by any measure or review of performance. In October 2003, a new provincial government was elected with a mandate and commitment to transform the school system. Wise individuals, who had been watching the United States jump from one fad or pedagogical ideology to another for well over seventy-five years, knew what NOT to do. Canada chose to focus on capacity building, fostering a formula for developing its teachers. (Unlike other industrialized nations, especially those that are the highest-achieving, the United States lacks a systematic approach to recruiting, preparing, and retaining teachers.[4])

With capacity building, a school or school district can become effective within a short period of time. Improvements began within a year. After four years, Ontario's nine hundred high schools showed an increase in graduation rates from 68 percent to 80 percent, and among those taking an extra year to earn their diploma, that number climbed to 86.5 percent.

A focus on capacity building allows teachers to reach their potential as effective and successful teachers in a short amount of time.

Ontario has climbed into the top tier of international rankings in the international **PISA** tests within the past four to five years. Ontario now ranks in the top ten for math, science, and reading.

Ontario has built the capacity of their teachers with professional development that supports leadership and instructional effectiveness.

Since the greatest assets of a school are its teachers and administrators, high-performing systems make capacity building the major focus. It begins with academically rigorous teacher education programs.

Capacity building requires robust, collaborative, professional development opportunities that are job-embedded and teacher-led.

There is a large population of immigrants in Canada who are eager to succeed. These migrant families want their children to excel at school, and the students are motivated to learn. There is a systematic effort to improve literacy with well-trained staff and resources such as school libraries, testing, and assessment to identify schools or individuals who are struggling. This has resulted in relatively little difference between advantaged and disadvantaged students.

The morale of teachers and principals in Canada is as strong as it has ever been, and there is far less new teacher attrition.

Induction in Poland

Before 2000, only half of the rural citizenry in Poland finished primary school. Now international scores in education rank Poland ahead of the United States. **Andreas Schleicher** at the Organization for Economic Cooperation and Development (O.E.C.D.) reported that Poland in less than a decade raised the literacy skills of its fifteen-year-olds by the equivalent of almost a school year.[5]

They did this by engaging teachers in the development of their new teacher colleagues to provide a highly effective and sustainable form of professional learning. New teachers are inducted into a content-rich core curriculum to

- acquire a body of knowledge covering facts, rules, theories, and practices;
- acquire the ability to use the knowledge gained in carrying out tasks and solving problems; and
- develop mindsets and attitudes which determine efficient and responsible functioning in the modern world.

Teachers in Polish secondary schools are rigorously trained to teach in multiple subject areas.

Chapter 8: High-Performing School Systems • 67

Induction in Shanghai, China

The world was shocked when the 2009 PISA results were published and Shanghai, China, emerged as number one in the world.

In Shanghai, all beginning teachers are immediately engaged in collaborative lesson preparation groups and teaching research groups. These groups involve new and veteran teachers in discussing and analyzing the lessons they are teaching, similar to the lesson study used in Japan.

A beginning teacher's career begins immediately as a member of a teaching-research group, which provides a forum for discussion of teaching techniques. Each teacher, new or experienced, must observe at least eight lessons (most observe more) a semester. It is very common for teachers to enter the classrooms of other teachers and discuss their observations. The conversations help new teachers acquire the language and norms of public discourse about teaching, which become a natural part of the fabric of any teacher's professional life. No special arrangements need to be made, for schools and teaching are organized to allow for such open observations. The method is so universal that everyone sees its wisdom and believes in its efficacy. **The most critical factor is that the lesson is critiqued, not the teacher.**

In Shanghai the evaluation of teachers is based on how teachers develop students' learning habits, not their test scores. Teachers are evaluated holistically on their participation in collaborative professional development and lesson study. The system works well because teachers get to see one another teach a great deal. Teaching is very public in Shanghai. **Teachers receive training in how to observe one another's classrooms.** This practice puts a subtle pressure on teachers to improve since, in principle, anyone can walk into any class at any time. A weekly system of teacher development—led by the school's master teachers—helps to develop the teaching skills of newer teachers.

All teachers are expected to
- diagnose student learning,
- develop effective lesson plans,
- reflect critically on their practice, and
- conduct research-oriented teaching.

Time is structured in a teacher's schedule to engage in high-quality professional development with their colleagues. They meet in research groups three hours a week, and all teachers are assigned to at least one group. They give demonstration lessons, share their lessons, and help underachieving schools. Lessons are recorded, and teachers can access the archive of past lessons for help in preparing lessons. Teaching thus becomes community property, not owned privately by one teacher, but shared by all.

Finally, Shanghai has placed a major focus on increasing equity in student achievement. It has done so, in part, through a policy of rotating master teachers and of sharing curriculum materials and teaching practices between stronger schools and those in poorer or more rural parts of the province. There is an empowered-management program that contracts high-performing schools to work with low-performing schools—usually for a two-year period—in order to turn around their performance. **Administrators and teachers volunteer to move between schools developing effective practices.** In this way they demonstrate their leadership and ability to succeed with diverse students and circumstances.

They are motivated to do so because teachers cannot get a raise in salary or promotion unless they can show that they can succeed in a challenging situation. However, the challenge is reduced because they have a cohort of fellow teachers and administrators who want to prove their mettle too, and who bring their professional capacity and shared commitment with them.

Thomas Friedman, author of *The World Is Flat*, did not mince words after a visit to Shanghai, finding there was "no secret" to the province's rapid rise in PISA rankings just "a deep commitment to teacher training, peer-to-peer learning, and constant professional development."[6]

Commonalities

The induction programs in schools of high-performing countries have three major similarities.

1. **Comprehensive structure.** Their respective induction approaches are highly structured, rigorous, and seriously monitored. Their leadership personnel—staff developers, administrators, instructors, and coaches—have well-defined roles.

2. **Professional learning.** The induction programs focus on professional learning to deliver growth and expertise to their teachers. They achieve this with an organized, sustained professional development system with many components during induction and continuing throughout a teacher's career.

3. **Collaboration.** Collaboration is the forte of high-performing schools. Collaborative group work is understood, fostered, and accepted as part of the teaching culture. There are shared experiences, shared practices, shared tools, and a shared language among all colleagues. And it is the function of the induction phase to engender this sense of group identity and treat new teachers as colleagues and cohorts.

What stands out about high-performing schools is that they have the smallest gaps between their strongest and weakest teachers. Good teaching is fostered throughout the school. **Teachers are never abandoned in their classrooms.** Collaboration is structured into the school day, and teachers usually meet regularly to jointly plan and develop curriculum. They participate in problem-solving groups that are involved in a cycle of planning, action, reflection.

High-performing systems first recruit the best possible people to become teachers. They are trained and continue to be trained during their career. There is **Continuous Professional Development** (CPD), an unwavering focus on training and supporting teachers, from their preservice work through retirement.

Teachers in high-performing countries perceive themselves as professionals who have both the obligation and the responsibility to plan, implement, and evaluate the outcomes of their work.

Comparison of Induction Activities in the World

Finland, Japan, Shanghai, China and Ontario, Canada	United States

Comprehensive Structure

• Highly structured, comprehensive, rigorous, seriously monitored • Teacher joins a culture/a community of practice/a larger system of teacher learning. • Organized induction team with a leader • Sustained process for two to five years • A pervasive culture committed to assisting beginning teachers • Well-defined roles of leadership personnel	• Sporadic, incoherent, lacks alignment, no adequate follow-up • New teacher typically treated as second-class citizen • Mentors are assigned to be "guides-by-the-side." • Induction non-existent in many school districts

Professional Learning

• Preservice, induction, and professional development flow seamlessly from one phase to the next. • Involves many people and components • Formal public lessons where lesson (not teacher) is criticized. • Variety and range of induction activities • Out-of-school training components • Open classroom visitations	• Mentors react (not proactive) to new teacher's day-to-day survival. • Principal defers support to a mentor. • Sporadic

Collaboration

• Collaborative (group) work • New teachers treated as colleagues and cohorts • Teaching is community property, shared by all. • Practice groups • Research groups/collaborative lesson planning • Lesson preparation groups • Teaching research/action research groups • Teachers are didacticians.	• Mentoring is one-on-one. • New teachers operate in isolation.

Professionally trained teachers are empowered to use their knowledge and skills to deliver the best possible instruction for every student.

Teachers have been trained in research skills so that they know how to work cooperatively with other teachers to improve instruction for student success. They are "partners in reform," ready to learn from one another—working with administrators and policy leaders to create the kind of professional learning systems that support effective teaching for 21st century schools.

In high-performing countries, you can only become an administrator when you can prove that you are a good teacher. Successful teachers may be promoted to department head and can take part in professional development and training to take on leadership roles in the school and the school system later in their careers. Principals are promoted from within the profession after they have shown that they are superior, effective teachers. The principal is constantly building the capacity of teachers to be more and more effective in teaching students a content-rich curriculum.

INDUCTION = UNLOCKING POTENTIAL

High-performing education systems stress the development of effective teachers through comprehensive induction programs, collaborative practices, and continuous professional development.

Share What You Do

If your school, school district, region, or country has an induction system for developing teacher capacity, please share it with us at HWong@HarryWong.com. Your success will help others develop theirs.

Endnotes

[1] Michael Barker and Mona Mourshed, *How the World's Best-Performing School Systems Come Out on Top* (McKinsey & Company: Insights on Education, September 1, 2007).

[2] Desiree Carver-Thomas and Linda Darling-Hammond, *Teacher Turnover: Why It Matters and What We Can Do About It* (Palo Alto, CA: Learning Policy Institute, August 16, 2017).

[3] "Students in Japan Clean Their Own Classrooms and School Toilets and the Reason Is Incredible," *India Today*, May 6, 2018, https://www.indiatoday.in/education-today/featurephilia/story/students-in-japan-clean-their-own-classrooms-and-school-toilets-and-the-reason-is-incredible-1227619-2018-05-06.

[4] Linda Darling-Hammond, *Recruiting and Retaining Teachers* (Stewart, OH: The Forum for Education and Democracy, March, 2015).

[5] Sam Dillon, "Many Nations Passing U.S. in Education," *The New York Times*, March 10, 2010, https://www.nytimes.com/2010/03/10/education/10educ.html.

[6] Thomas Friedman, "The Shanghai Secret," *The New York Times*, October 22, 2013, https://www.nytimes.com/2013/10/23/opinion/friedman-the-shanghai-secret.html.

9 High-Performing Companies

New employees are trained immediately so that they can successfully accomplish the requirements of their job.

Embedded Training

Businesses train new employees. If this is so obvious, you may choose to skip reading this chapter. But before you do, why isn't it apparent that schools should do the same?

If you are hired as a new employee in a company, the first thing you ask is, "What do you want me to do?" Conversely, if you manage a business you will tell a new employee what to do.

Airline Pilots

Pilot training is recurrent, meaning it is ongoing throughout a pilot's career. When a pilot changes seats, like from Copilot to Captain or changes to a new aircraft like from a Boeing 737 to a Boeing 777, additional training occurs.

Training is generally a little more than two weeks of ground school followed by a long written and oral exam. The next part of instruction is a series of periods in a simulator of eight hours each for another two weeks.

After passing a final simulator exam, the pilot flies on regularly scheduled passenger trips for twenty-five hours with an instructor pilot. Six months later the pilot is back in training for a recurrent period with additional home study, which is tested before reporting for recurrent training. **Passengers can relax on a flight knowing the pilot and copilot have been trained to know what to do.**

> Not to provide induction is like asking a pilot to learn how to fly while taking a plane load of passengers up for the first time.

Starbucks

Starbucks puts new baristas—a person who is specially trained in the making and serving of coffee drinks—through a strict training regime in their first two to four weeks on the job. During this time, new recruits complete at least twenty-four hours of training. Starbucks' training doesn't just focus exclusively on the mechanics of the position. Since the company understands that their employees are an extension of the brand, initial training includes sessions on coffee history, coffee knowledge, customer service, retail skills,

72 • THE New Teacher Induction Book

and a four-hour workshop about how to brew the perfect cup of coffee.

Barista training is called a **"Learning Journey."** It consists of workbook assignments and technology-based training at the manager's workstation. Topics covered include First Impressions (a review of Starbucks culture, history, benefits, and job expectations), customer service, coffee, beverage recipes, Point of Sale (POS) and cash handling, and merchandise selling. New baristas are paired with a Learning Coach who reviews workbook assignments and their work alongside a partner during scheduled shifts. Learning coaches have completed coach training and can be a store manager or shift supervisor. New baristas have a formal performance review after six months.

Starbucks encourages its employees, who are called partners, to keep in mind its mission statement, monitor management decisions, and submit comments and questions if they encounter anything that runs counter to the company's mission statement. Employees submit about 200 such Mission Review queries a month, and a two-person team considers and responds to each one.

Starbucks has one of the highest job-satisfaction ratings in the industry. **Customers can count on** a coffee that is served at Starbucks to be expertly prepared by a partner who has been trained in how to make a cup of coffee that reflects the mission of the company.

Starbucks Closes Every Store

On a Tuesday night in February 2008, Starbucks closed all of its stores for three hours to review everyone on how to make the perfect cup of espresso. As Starbucks said, "This is not about training. This is about consistently giving the customer a coffee they can count on every day, all day, all week."

Domino's Pizza

Domino's most visible employees are its drivers. They receive training for ten days before they become the face of the business.

Day 1: New Employee Orientation
- Completion of paperwork for new employees
- Introduction to the history, locations, rules, and standard operating procedures
- View safe driving video

Chapter 9: High-Performing Companies • 73

Days 2–4: Store and Product Orientation
- Store tour
- Product orientation
- Mock phone orders

Days 5–7: Delivery Training
- Driver trainer explains order routing and delivery procedures.
- New driver shadows trainer for one to two shifts.
- Mock deliveries begin in store.

Days 8–9: Beginning Delivery
- New driver is in control of deliveries while trainer observes.
- New driver must call times in and out of door.

Day 10: Driver
- Driver begins independent delivery runs.

As the largest pizza company in the world, Domino's leadership believes in doing the right thing and championing its drivers by delivering great-tasting pizza to its customers' doors.

Walmart

The essence of **Walmart's** success is that they refer to their workers as associates and believe that they are the greatest asset of the company. They cannot succeed without the continued support of their associates. To do this, they invest in their associates through training and skills development so that all jobs lead to careers.

Walmart is the world's largest retailer. With 4,500 stores in the United States alone, it has 1.2 million store associates—not workers—who are the backbone of the business. Every new Walmart employee and manager goes through an induction process simply known as the **"Academy"** inside some of the larger Walmarts. The Academy is a classroom in the back of a store replete with ranks of desktop computers and tablets loaded with software, in front of walls decorated with trademark blue and yellow graphics with upbeat messages. Every new associate trainee is wearing the Walmart vest so everyone belongs to "the Walmart family" the moment that they become a Walmart associate.

Depending on the responsibility of the new employee, the training can range from one to six weeks of hands-on, applicable instruction. But that's just on the surface. On a deeper level, the Walmart Academy invests in its people to make them better at their jobs and better in their everyday life. **It is reassuring that Walmart gives its associates the tools and skills they need to professionally serve their customers and the personal growth they need to advance in their careers.**

The Cheesecake Factory

Newly hired staff members at **The Cheesecake Factory** attend orientation lasting four to five hours. The time covers a discussion of general information that includes a welcome, a review of the handbook with important policies and procedures, a tour of the facility, completing new hire paperwork, and a meeting with the general manager and Lead Trainer.

The Lead Trainer reviews the new hire's training schedule, which consists of five days of on-the-job training (OJT) of approximately forty hours. The new hire trains with a Designated Trainer (DT). A Designated Trainer is an hourly staff member who has been certified as a subject matter expert in that position. (They are not untrained mentors!) Throughout the OJT, the new employee and the DT work side by side. There are frequent quizzes, both orally and written, depending on the position, over a forty-hour period. On the last day of training, the DT validates the skills that the new hire can perform to ascertain competency.

Staff members are retrained twice a year and if staff members do well, they may be eligible for merit increase and cross-training in another area. Staff members can become a DT after six months of service. They attend a one day **"Train the Trainer"** class, which focuses on training skills, methods, communication, and coaching. In another six months, they can be eligible for a New Restaurant Opener position to help open a new restaurant (given a per diem and paid at a higher rate) where they help supervise and train new staff members. **At the The Cheesecake Factory, training is ongoing and is conducted by all levels of management.**

McDonald's

If you visit a particular **McDonald's** on a regular basis it becomes apparent that you rarely see the same employee again. The average fast-food worker, such as at McDonald's, stays for two and one-half months. To satisfy staffing needs, they hire the gamut of applicants—immigrants, senior citizens, school dropouts, and physically-challenged people. Yet, each employee knows what to do and does it with speed.

How do they do it? McDonald's has a well-organized and comprehensive training program. Every employee goes through a **"Station Observation Checklist,"** which comprises a list of tasks that are to be performed at each station or job, such as food preparation processes, customer interaction, sanitation practices, and maintenance tasks, while training under the instruction from a senior manager.

After a brief orientation, which is the only lecture-like component involved in basic staff training, new employees are partnered with trained, senior staff members, shoulder-to-shoulder, to learn hands-on the eleven different workstations in the restaurant.

McDonald's has standardized its training and has established **Hamburger University**, a global training center dedicated to developing individuals' skills and knowledge in restaurant operation procedures—quality, service, cleanliness, and value. There are numerous training centers scattered around the world. **You have no fear of going into a McDonald's anywhere in the world as all employees have been trained the same way so they can deliver a consistent, customer outcome—one that you feel comfortable experiencing.**

The Most Critical Position

> A teacher is one of the most critical positions anyone will ever hold.

Successful businesses train employees with a comprehensive, coherent, and sustained program. Even local, small businesses—dentists, real estate offices, and grocery stores—train all new workers, from the day an employee joins a company or team until that person leaves.

New hires in most businesses are given in-depth training that enables them to do their job as their job descriptions dictate. While it's true that a good cup of coffee can make all the difference in the morning and a good meal delivered to your house or restaurant table can bring a smile to one's face, none of the employees at these fine establishments will imprint the life of a child so greatly as a teacher.

Perhaps the United States teaching establishment should look to the successes of businesses in other industries for models. Employees are trained when they first begin a new job so that they are able to conduct themselves according to the policies of the company. They are taught so they can successfully accomplish the requirements of their job. They are guided so they share the same mission, goals, and objectives as others in their company.

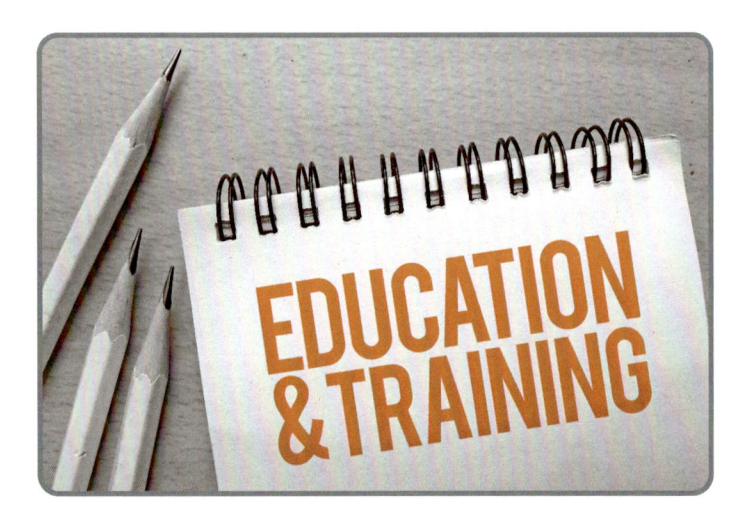

Whether a new person hired for the first time in the industry or a new person hired is new to the company, everyone is trained to the mission, goals, and objectives of the business.

Next to parenting, being a teacher is one of the most critical life-affecting positions anyone will ever hold. Domino's, Starbucks, United Airlines, and other successful companies understand the importance of training in building effective employees, **yet most school systems in the United States do not.**

Isn't it ironic that the teaching profession does a poor job of teaching its own, and we have to look to others for successful training models yet fail to implement them?

Return on Investment

The greatest tragedy is the annual loss from not harnessing the potential intellectual capacity of new teachers.

A Coach's Return on Investment

Amanda Bivens,
Instructional Coach

As of the 2022–2023 school year, **Amanda Bivens has coached fifty-four teachers, and ALL are still in teaching.** There has been no attrition under her coaching. She not only has saved the Tennessee district money; she has made money for them. Businesses would call this a good **Return on Investment** (ROI).

In the infinite wisdom of the administrators in the Dyer County Schools, they have hired a K–2 coach, 3–5 coach, middle school coach, high school coach, and literacy coach. All of the coaches work together daily and share information.

One of these coaches is **Amanda Bivens**. Amanda is an Instructional Coach. Her major responsibility is to coach third-, fourth-, and fifth-grade teachers, new teachers, and strengthen veteran teachers for three years.

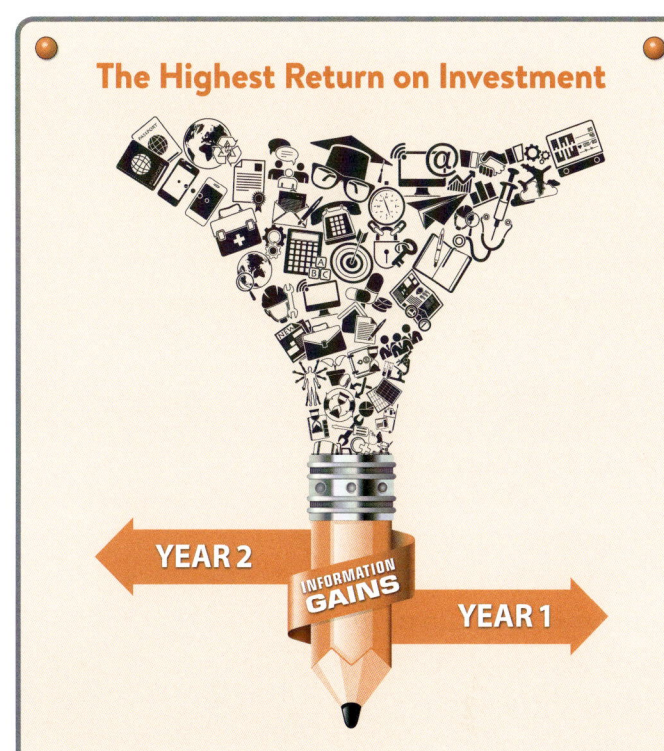

The Highest Return on Investment

Teachers learn 50 percent of what they come to know about teaching in their first year in the classroom and half as much again in the second year, and it becomes relatively flat after that. The majority of those teachers (62 percent) in their first year who had the lowest effects on students are the same teachers who had the lowest effect on students five years later.

Conversely, the majority of those teachers (73 percent) with the greatest effects in their first year are the same teachers with the highest effects five years later.[1]

Therefore, the greatest return on investment is what new teachers learn from their new teacher induction program.

Chapter 10: Return on Investment • 77

Amanda shares . . .

"As an Instructional Coach, I tell my newly hired teachers that being an effective teacher doesn't just happen, and contrary to some beliefs, it isn't a teacher who has the most experience, highest degree, or prettiest classroom. It is a teacher who has
1. good classroom management skills,
2. teaches for mastery of content, and
3. positive expectations for each student's potential and success.

Education, on the other hand, churns through programs and fads believing that these will create student achievement—with NO return on investment.

A New Teacher's Response

"I want to start off by saying how lucky I am to have Amanda as an Instructional Coach. Amanda was there when I needed her for teaching advice or when I just needed to vent to someone. She never once hesitated to help me!

Emily Jones, New Teacher

As a first-year teacher, I was nervous about many things. However, the two main things were classroom management and having the resources I needed to perform to be the best teacher I could be. I teach fourth grade and was blessed to have a great homeroom class, but my other two classes were trouble. One class was full of behavioural problems while the other had several special education students. Within the first few weeks of school, I knew if I wanted to have a successful year, I would need to turn the situation around as fast as possible.

I reached out to Amanda and we came up with a plan. Amanda suggested she come teach the behaviour problem class and demonstrate how to conduct accountable talk[2] in the classroom. I instantly fell in love with accountable talk and the students did too. I feel as though I was able to have a successful year with that class because of Amanda's coaching and techniques.

When I got the results of our first assessment and saw my lowest class's average was higher than the district—I was overjoyed! The first person I told was Amanda!

I feel as though I had a very successful first year of teaching. Being a first-year teacher, I had to have three observations this school year, one announced and two unannounced. I made a score of four out of five on all my observations! I am very blessed to have Amanda as my Instructional Coach and I am looking forward to having her as a colleague for many years to come!

The Cost of Teacher Attrition

New teachers reach over four million students each year.

Currently, 168,900 new teachers enter the classroom, reaching an estimated 4.2 million students. At the same time, roughly half a million U.S. teachers either move or leave the profession each year—attrition that **costs the United States up to $2.2 billion annually**, according to a report from the **Alliance for Excellent Education**.[3]

Every school day, over a thousand teachers leave the field of teaching. Another thousand teachers change schools, many in pursuit of better working conditions. And these figures do not include the teachers who retire.

This high turnover rate disproportionately affects high-poverty schools and seriously compromises the nation's capacity to ensure that all students have access to skilled, effective teachers.

Every day more than 1,000 teachers leave the profession.

This checklist of items itemizes the cost of turnover in a school district. These calculations will easily reach 150 percent of the employee's annual compensation figure. In addition, the cost will be significantly higher (200 percent to 250 percent of annual compensation) for administrator positions. To put this into perspective, let's assume the average salary of a teacher is $65,000 per year. Taking the cost of turnover at 150 percent of salary, the cost of turnover is then $97,500 per employee who leaves the school. **For the mid-sized district of 1,000 teachers that has a 10 percent annual rate of turnover, the annual cost of turnover is $9,750,000—nearly ten million dollars!**

Can you imagine what your district could do for its teachers with nearly $10 million dollars?

What's interesting is that the costs of turnover are <u>hidden</u> in mounds of teacher records, school data, and district financial information making its real cost unknown to parents, the public, and the policymakers. Parents and teachers never see this cost because the direct costs are buried and spread across human resources, business services, deputy superintendent, chief financial officer, payroll supervisor, benefits clerk, and staff development budgets. **School district budgets do not include a single line item for teacher turnover costs.**[4]

To reveal the costs, consider this collection of costs.

Costs Due to a Person Leaving

- The substitute(s) who fills in while the position is vacant.
- Lost productivity at a minimum of 50 percent of the person's compensation and benefits cost for each week the position is vacant, even if there are people performing the work.
- Conducting an exit interview to include the time of the person conducting the interview and the time of the person leaving.
- The administrative costs of stopping payroll, benefit deductions, benefit enrollments, and the cost of the various forms needed to process a resigning employee.
- Time the district has spent training (if at all) the teacher who is leaving.
- Lost knowledge, skills, and contacts that the person who is leaving is taking out of your school and district.

Recruitment Costs

- Advertising, agency costs, and Internet posting incurred per listing.
- Recruiter's time to understand the position requirements, develop and implement a

sourcing strategy, review candidate's backgrounds, prepare for interviews, conduct interviews, prepare candidate assessments, conduct reference checks, developing candidate interview schedules, make any travel arrangements for out-of-town candidates, make the employment offer, and notify successful and unsuccessful candidates.
- Administrative cost of handling, processing, and responding to the average number of resumes considered for each opening.
- Number of hours spent by the recruiter interviewing candidates.
- Drug screens, educational and criminal background checks, and other reference checks used, especially if these tasks are outsourced.
- Pre-employment tests to help assess a candidate's skills, abilities, reasoning, aptitude, attitude, values, and behaviors.

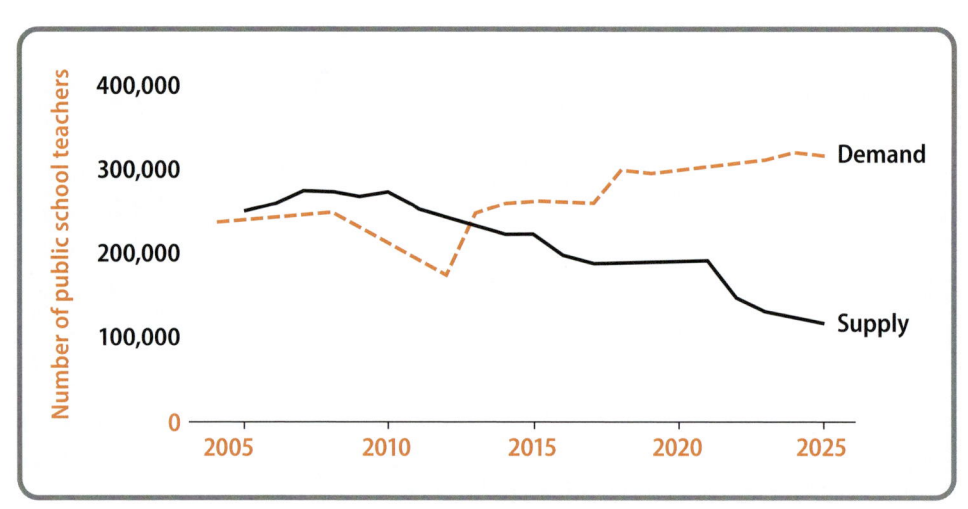

Training Costs

- Orientation (if there is one) in terms of the new person's salary and the cost of the people conducting the orientation.
- Induction training (if there is any) and the cost of the people conducting the training.
- Training materials (if any) needed to deliver the training.

New Hire Costs

- Putting the new teacher on the payroll.
- Establishing computer access and security passwords—identification cards, cellphone, laptop, computer, email accounts, and any other items needed by the new teacher.

- Replenishing classroom supplies because the materials from the previous teacher are nowhere to be found.

When teachers leave, policymakers and administrators simply focus on recruiting new teachers, ignoring the cost—and the constant churn simply repeats itself as if there is an endless supply of teachers and money because that is the way it has always been done.

There is no longer an endless supply of teachers or money.

The task of recruiting teachers from an endless supply no longer exists and has not existed since before 2015.

This scenario is different in countries like Finland, Singapore, and Korea where they can select from the top 10 to 25 percent of the high school and college graduates who vie to become teachers. Once they become teachers in these high-performing countries, 3 to 4 percent of teachers leave the profession each year, usually for retirement.

In the United States, the annual teacher attrition is about 8 percent for those who leave education with the same portion of teachers who change schools resulting in an overall annual turnover rate of 16 percent. Roughly nine out of every ten teachers hired each year are replacing colleagues who left voluntarily. Teacher turnover is even higher in Title I schools where the turnover rate is nearly 50 percent greater than other schools. Rates among Title I math and science teachers are nearly 70 percent greater. These factors are further magnified in schools with a larger population of students of color.[5,6]

The Hidden Turnover Cost

While the actual turnover costs can't be quantified, there is another cost that is not so hidden. It is the cost of educating teachers (if any such programs exist) in underperforming schools.

When students start a new school year, far too many are greeted by substitute teachers and others who are unprepared for their jobs, as teacher shortages continue to hinder the ability of districts to find fully prepared teachers to fill its classrooms.

Each year, more than 100,000 classrooms in the U.S. are being staffed by instructors who are uncertified for their assignments and lack the content background and training to teach their classes. These classrooms are disproportionately in schools serving mostly students from low-income families and students of color. In some key subjects, like math, science, and special education, districts of every type and in nearly every state feel the shortage.

In addition to underqualified teachers, there are at least 5,000 unfilled vacancies during the school year. These numbers understate total shortages because some states have only partial survey data or report uncertified teachers only in core areas and not all subjects.

Not only are underprepared teachers less effective on average, they are also two to three times more likely to leave teaching than fully prepared teachers, creating a revolving door that makes solving shortages an uphill, financial climb.

New teachers, especially in urban schools, are significantly less experienced and less qualified than teachers in other schools. This results in little opportunity for developing supportive professional relationships among the staff. Thus, successful urban schools need stable teacher populations and continuing instructional leadership.[7]

When schools are continually losing teachers, relationships are disrupted, professional development investments are thrown away, curriculum and school improvement efforts are derailed, and student achievement suffers.

All too often, the solution to teacher shortages in underperforming schools is to focus on recruiting warm bodies just to have a teacher (or adult) in the classrooms, **even though improving retention is the most critical issue to solving shortages in the long run**.

So, school districts with a high new-teacher attrition rate do what the great majority of schools do—they hire a teacher, give that teacher an assignment, and expect the individual to go forth and teach. Imagine the costs and frustration of continually rehiring another teacher with this system.

Low-performing schools rarely close the student achievement gap because the teacher quality gap is never closed.

These schools are constantly reassembling the staff.

An inordinate amount of the school's capital—both human and financial—is consumed by the constant process of hiring and replacing beginning teachers who leave before they have mastered the ability to create a successful learning culture for their students.

Instead of reassembling staffs, districts should be reconstituting its staff with an induction program that will produce effective teachers.

Schools and districts continue to hire replacement bodies and hope in earnest that they will be able to teach classes in an effective manner—without being taught how to establish effective classrooms and create effective instruction.

Trapped in a chronic cycle of teacher hiring and replacement these schools drain their districts of precious dollars that could be better spent to improve teaching quality and student achievement.

In both small and large districts, the costs of recruiting, hiring, and training a replacement teacher are substantial. In 2020 figures, in Granville County, North Carolina, the cost of each teacher who left the district was just under $12,000. In the small rural district of Jemez Valley, New Mexico, the cost per teacher who left was $5,100. In Milwaukee, the average cost per lost teacher was $19,000. In a very large district like

I Was Never Told How I Fit Into the School

> *In elementary school, no one ever picked me. That rejection and its resulting hurt stayed with me through life. So, when I became a teacher, I vowed never to allow my students to be rejected. But how could I do that when rejection was the initial experience I encountered on my very first day as a brand-new teacher? I was not introduced to the staff. I was not shown to my room. I was not told how to get supplies. I was not even shown the bathrooms! I was not told how I would fit in with the staff and how I could contribute.*
>
> *Needless to say, I left after my first year. Looking back, the reason is obvious. There was no culture at this school, so I could not "fit in" to something that did not exist. It was simply a place where people worked—and I use that word loosely—behind closed doors.*
>
> A frustrated teacher
> Who chose to stay anonymous

When a teacher leaves, so does the money used to recruit and train that teacher. Districts can save money by saving its teachers.

82 • THE New Teacher Induction Book

Chicago, the average cost was $21,000 per teacher. The total cost of turnover in the Chicago Public Schools is estimated to be over $110 million. It is clear that thousands of dollars fly out the window each time a teacher leaves.

At-risk schools spend already sparse dollars on teacher turnover. Low-performing, high-minority, and high-poverty schools expend limited resources on teacher turnover. Because teacher attrition rates in these types of schools are chronically high, turnover costs become a drain on school leadership and on already scarce resources that could otherwise be invested to improve teaching effectiveness and student growth.

With 46 percent of all new teachers in the United States leaving the profession within five years, an at-risk school is in a constant cycle of rebuilding its staff.

Beginning teachers are particularly vulnerable because they are more likely than their more experienced colleagues to be assigned low-performing students. Despite the added challenges that come with teaching children and adolescents with higher needs, most new teachers are given little professional support, feedback, or demonstration of what it takes to help their students succeed.

In addition to the exorbitant teacher turnover costs, student performance may also be negatively impacted by teacher turnover, especially in districts with consistently high turnover rates.

Even more important, we neglect the human cost for new teachers who invest time and resources to become teachers. They want to succeed, but then are put into at-risk environments.

Teaching Is Unique

In no other profession other than teaching are
inexperienced,
untrained, and
untried
beginners left to their own devices
and allowed to have autonomous responsibility
to make substantive professional decisions.

With a lawyer, doctor, reporter, or peace officer, there is a structure that provides
training,
daily guidance,
tutelage,
and
supervision.[8]

Dennis Evans

> The greatest tragedy
> in education today
> is the annual loss
> from not harnessing
> the potential intellectual capacity
> of new teachers.

Instead of looking for a solution, the cycle repeats itself each year as administrators scurry and spend more money to hire replacements—who will receive no training—who also leave within the first few years of employment. There is tremendous potential inside the raw material of new teachers, but these diamonds in the rough are being turned back into coal and cast aside. Money is being wasted, and students are suffering.

The Remedy

The difference between school districts with high turnover and those with low turnover is quite simple. School districts with a low teacher attrition rate have an organized, multiyear, sustained program to train, support, and retain new recruits. This process is called **New Teacher Induction**, the purpose of which is to train, support, and then retain these effective teachers.

Studies show that the best return on investment is spent on training and developing effective teachers. This expenditure yields greater student achievement. Money spent on other school resources does not produce notable results.[9]

Implementing strategies to retain qualified teachers must become a precedence.

The most cost-effective way to increase student achievement is to improve teacher competency, which can be achieved at a fraction of the cost of reducing class size or spending money on yet another flavor-of-the-month program or technology.

Studies confirm that teacher quality has the greatest impact on student achievement. Therefore, it makes sense to strive not only to attract good teachers but also to train, support, and retain them. When we retain good teachers, our schools become more effective, and student achievement improves.

Districts need to invest in new teacher induction programs that have been proven to increase teacher retention and improve student achievement. The costs of such programs could be offset by the savings achieved through decreases in the costs of attrition and turnover.[10]

- An induction process is the best way to send a message to new teachers that you value them and want them to succeed and stay.

- Every new teacher is a human resource, a person who has invested years in preparing for a life dedicated to helping young people.

- We have a responsibility to ensure that new teachers will learn and succeed, just as we have a responsibility to ensure that every student will learn and succeed.

- New teachers must be trained if we want them to succeed. Without training, new teachers are at a greater risk of failing early in their careers—a loss to their students and to the profession.

The solution has been right in front of us all along. Rather than allocate scarce funds for expensive efforts to recruit and replace teachers, money can be saved by training, supporting, and thus keeping the many capable hopeful teachers who truly can and will make a difference. Whether we consider the direct costs or the hidden costs associated with replacing a teacher, we must acknowledge and act to prevent the slow but steady leak that is depleting school budgets and hobbling efforts to make our schools truly effective. The cost of teacher turnover is high, both economically and emotionally. **Implementing strategies to retain qualified teachers must become a priority.**

Districts must offer an induction program that is comprehensive, coherent, and sustained to our new teachers.

- The school districts can't afford the replacement costs.
- The new teachers can't afford the lack of training and support.
- Most important, students can't afford to be taught by untrained teachers.

Amanda Bivens is working with only **ONE** new grade 3–5 teacher this school year. Why? The Dyer County process works for retraining new hires. All fifty-four of Amanda's previously coached new teachers are thriving in the district—elevating the achievement of students and keeping money in the district's coffers to be spent on enhancing education.

Endnotes

[1] Allison Atteberry, Susanna Loeb, and James Wyckoff, "Do First Impressions Matter? Predicting Early Career Teacher Effectiveness," *AERA Open* 1, no. 3 (2015).

[2] See *THE Classroom Instruction Book* page 205 for how to use the accountable talk strategy.

[3] "Teacher Attrition Costs United States Up to $2.2 Billion Annually, Says New Alliance Report," *Alliance for Excellent Education* (2014).

[4] Eliah Watlington, Robert Shockley, Paul Guglielmino, and Rivka Felsher, "The High Cost of Leaving: An Analysis of the Cost of Teacher Turnover," *Journal of Education Finance* (January 2010).

[5] Emma Garcia and Elaine Weiss, "U.S. Schools Struggle to Hire and Retain Teachers," *Economic Policy Institute* (April 2019).

[6] Desiree Carver-Thomas and Linda Darling-Hammond, "Teacher Turnover: Why It Matters and What We Can Do About It," *Learning Policy Institute* (August 16, 2017).

[7] Frederick M. Hampton and T. L. Purcell, "The Prefect Storm in Urban Schools: Student, Teacher, and Principal Transience," *ERS Spectrum* (Spring 2005).

[8] Dennis L. Evans, "Assistance for Underqualified Teachers," *Education Week* (February 3, 1999).

[9] Ronald F. Ferguson, "Paying for Public Education: New Evidence on How and Why Money Matters," *Harvard Journal of Legislation* 28 (Summer 1991): 465–498.

[10] Gary Barnes, Edward Crowe, and Benjamin Schaefer, "The Cost of Teacher Turnover in Five School Districts," *National Commission on Teaching and America's Future* (2007).

Developing New Teachers

11 First Five Minutes of the First Day
Preparation for the first day of teaching is essential to ensuring continued success. **87**

12 Induction Program Essentials
An induction program teaches effective classroom management and effective classroom instruction. **97**

13 Recruiting New Teachers
The best induction programs teach new teachers how to deliver instruction with a clear understanding of what students need to learn. **108**

14 How to Start and Sustain an Induction Program
An effective induction program is attainable and sustainable. **114**

Afterword **122**

11 First Five Minutes of the First Day

Preparation for the first day of teaching is essential to ensuring continued success.

Before the First Day of School

> The most important day of a new teacher's education is not graduation day. It's the first day of school.

Teaching begins instantly on the first day of school. Some twenty-five to thirty students will walk into the classroom. Not only does the teacher have to engage with these students, but there are materials, texts, technological equipment, and supplies to control and master. The teacher must take attendance and complete an absent-from-class form, record and deal with tardy students, handle bathroom or other "emergency" requests, and last but not least, collect student work, conduct instruction, give assignments, and connect with students.

There is a saying, "You only have one chance to make a first impression." The first day of school can give students such jitters they often can't sleep the night before. (This happens to teachers, too!) Entering a new school—starting a new school year—encountering new people in a classroom can all strike fear in a student. If the school is disorganized—with no "welcome" sign in the classroom indicating the name of the class and the teacher, no teacher when they walk into the classroom, the furniture in disarray, no seating chart—students' confidence and enthusiasm can be seriously undermined. It will be an uphill struggle for many weeks for teachers to regain the trust of their students, if ever.

Research shows that students who are given the opportunity to make comfortable transitions into the classroom and school and experience early success in learning tend to maintain and keep higher levels of social competence and academic achievement throughout their school years.[1]

Good teachers know this. They spend days and hours preparing for that most important day of the year, the first day of school. **Planning is the hallmark of success.**

A good induction program will prepare teachers for the first days of school. The program starts before the school year begins, not after beginning teachers are left floundering, not knowing how to start the first minute, the first day

Chapter 11: First Five Minutes of the First Day • 87

in the new school year. A culture of professional development is in place before teachers even see their first class.

As a successful chef or home cook knows, being organized and prepared before any cooking begins is the key to a successful outcome. Focus and time is lost if everything is not gathered and ready at the start. The restaurant industry calls this "mise en place," everything is in place before beginning.

Preparation is essential for success.

A set of blueprints is useless
after the building has collapsed.

A recipe is useless
after the cake has burned.

A map is useless
after you are lost.

Plans should be consulted
before embarking on an endeavor.

Without an induction program or adequate professional development, beginning teachers tend to develop coping strategies in order to survive in the classroom. This survival approach to teaching can quickly crystallize into inadequate teaching styles that these teachers then resort to throughout their career.

Untrained new teachers can quickly fall into the trap of just coping. That's when good people become bad teachers, a product of poor professional development.

The Beginning Determines the Rest

It's what a school does for a teacher at the beginning that determines what will happen to that teacher from that point onwards. If you knit, you know that the most important row is the first row. Start it incorrectly and you will have to rip the piece apart to start all over again. Painters spend days sanding, taping, and scaffolding before they even open the first can of paint. It's the only way to do the job successfully. Like a bricklayer, a teacher must carefully lay the classroom's groundwork on the first day, knowing that every moment afterwards will rest on this foundation.

The first row will determine how well the rest of the bricks are laid and the success of the project.

An induction program prepares teachers for what lies ahead on the first moment of teaching and every minute thereafter. It provides systems, methods, procedures, skills, training, practice, and support to inspire confidence and positive expectations. It helps new teachers avoid pitfalls; it helps them be informed, alert, and aware of their responsibilities and possibilities; it helps them feel poised and secure. It shapes novices into professionals who can hit the ground running.

The more training and professional development teachers receive, the more effective they are able to be from the beginning.

If your teachers find themselves in a school or district that does not have an induction program and they are left to their own devices, there are steps they can take to pave the way to eventual success. The first days of teaching will be less difficult and traumatic. Giving teachers a checklist without support is not an induction program. But, it's better than giving no direction at all.

Start of School Checklist

Walking into a room, you do not usually pay attention to the floor. But if the floor was missing you would.

Two Promising Teachers

Five Minutes Can Make or Break You

"I was hired as a brand-new teacher at this school. I showed up at the principal's office and was greeted by the school secretary. I never saw the principal. I was given the key to a room and had to find it on my own. No one greeted me or walked me to my room. The room was filthy with garbage all over and furniture askew, nothing that resembled a learning environment. I was introduced to no one. No one told me where to eat lunch, when to eat lunch, where the faculty restroom was, and where to find supplies. No one told me if there was a bell schedule, when school began, and when each period began and ended.

Now I know what was told to me in ed school, that the first day of school and the first five minutes of a class can make or break you.

A first-year teacher

Gone After One Year

Anthony, a newly hired teacher, received one day of orientation, during which he mostly filled out forms. No one officially welcomed him or the three other new teachers to the school.

By the time school started in this large urban school district, more than one thousand people had been handed classroom keys. They were directed to the most troubled schools. They had no educational experience, no guidance, no instruction, no induction, and scant support.

At the end of September of that year, one hundred new teachers had already quit. Six other teachers quit during the year at Anthony's school. Anthony struggled to control his classroom. At the end of the year almost all his students failed the state writing tests, and Anthony left teaching.

Chapter 11: First Five Minutes of the First Day • 89

It's the same with classroom management. Teachers who have a well-managed classroom have invisible procedures. The class just flows along smoothly with student learning. This is because they spend time during the first week of school organizing and structuring the classroom for student learning.

Imagine the success of a teacher who had been trained and had the skills, background, and knowledge to develop and implement a checklist for the first day of school.

- Classroom routines and procedures have been developed.
- Routines and procedures are posted neatly and are large enough to be read.
- Rules and consequences are posted.
- Heading sample is displayed.
- Professional honors, diplomas, and certificates are displayed.
- A consistent place is reserved for assignments with due dates.
- Student schedule is posted.
- An opening assignment or bellwork is used to start instruction.
- Relevant sponge activities are available to maximize instructional time.
- A signal to quiet class is taught and used as needed.
- The classroom is arranged to facilitate guided practice activities.
- The classroom environment conveys the message that learning is important.
- The home is contacted with positive calls or notes about students.

> *My greatest responsibility is to empower the students to become as independent as possible. Once they are able to perform the getting started procedure on their own, that allows me to work individually with the ones who might need extra help with lessons from the previous day.*
>
> Renee Tomita
> Oak Brook, Illinois

In a well-managed classroom, the teacher doesn't even need to be in the classroom and the students all know what to do.

A signal procedure will quiet the classroom in seconds.

The First Five Minutes

When class begins, getting students to work should take precedence. In fact, students have testified that the best classrooms are those where they are kept busy with learning, and the day flows smoothly.

Students thrive in organized environments with routines and consistency. Posting the daily agenda allows both you and your students to refer to it throughout the day. This keeps everyone on task and accountable for their time.

Effective teachers use procedures and rehearse the students in them so they follow the procedures automatically, enabling the class to start immediately and efficiently.

- The teacher greets students at the door.
- Students sit in their assigned seats.
- They go through their start-of-class routine.
- They look at the agenda.
- They begin the opening assignment.

While students are preparing for class and beginning their opening assignments, the teacher is taking attendance or doing whatever housekeeping tasks are needed. At the end of five minutes, instruction begins.

Maximizing the crucial first five minutes for secondary teachers is important, especially for those who see students for a limited amount of time each day.

Science

When students walk in the door, they go to the shelf where the papers they will need for the class period are stored. Papers are picked up and students find their seats. The daily agenda, objective, and bellwork assignment are always posted. Students know they are to begin working on the bellwork assignment. When they finish, they work on something else or wait quietly.

During this time, I take attendance and return papers (or a student helper returns papers). I point to the posted agenda and verbally announce it. I also use this time to give feedback on the previous assignment. Then we start the day.

Karen Rogers
Kansas

Communication Arts

Students walk into the room; retrieve their interactive notebooks; review the agenda, learning target, and essential question for the day (written on the whiteboard); and then journal write to the prompt on the Smartboard. Journal prompts often ask them to think about an idea connected to what we are learning about that day.

After five minutes (a timer is used), I often call on a few students to share their writing as we begin instruction.

Brandy Hackett
Moberly, Missouri

While most elementary teachers have students all day, they understand that every minute is still crucial and a learning opportunity.

First Grade

My first-grade students enter the classroom and begin a series of morning opening procedures: backpacks, home learning folder, lunch and snack money, notes, and morning assignment. During this time, I take the attendance; they listen to the principal's message; and they recite the "Pledge of Allegiance."

I can't stress enough how important procedures and routines are.

Many people do not believe that young children can follow procedures and routines. My classroom is proof that it works.

Maureen Conley
Central Islip, New York

Third Grade

> *When the bell rings, I greet my students on the blacktop. We walk to our classroom where I greet each student at the door with a handshake and eye contact, saying, "Good morning." It's a great way to start the day, showing respect for one another and making everyone feel welcome to our classroom.*
>
> *Once students enter, they do their morning duties of unpacking, taking attendance, and turning in homework. Then they start the bellwork assignment on the board.*
>
> *Our morning runs efficiently, and the day is off to a great start!*
>
> Sarah F. Jondahl
> Georgetown, Texas

Fifth Grade

> *When students enter my classroom, their daily Bell Ringer is projected on my board. The students are to take out their agendas and copy their homework.*
>
> *Students then place their homework assignments from the previous night on their desks. If the homework is not completed, they are to complete a missing assignment slip.*
>
> *To begin instruction for the day, students work on their daily oral language or reading comprehension assignment.*
>
> *Following this, students read silently in their independent reading books until the lesson begins (in a few minutes).*
>
> Megan Toujouse
> Covington, Louisiana

Jacinda Edwards of Indiana has an extensive **Classroom Management Plan** that she uses to prepare for the first day of school.

Before Students Arrive Checklist

- Communicate with parents or guardians my goals for the year and my excitement for having their children in my class.
- Mail all students a postcard that welcomes them to my class and expresses excitement for the upcoming school year. There will be instructions on the postcard telling students to bring the cards on the first day as their "tickets" to enter the classroom (extra postcards ready for new students who did not receive one).
- Make a sign showing my name, the room number, and the grade level and post it outside the room. Write this information on the front board in the classroom as well.
- Post a list of student names in order by first name inside the door.
- Have a dry erase board for lunch count posted directly inside the room to one side of the door with individual magnets for each child (each child's first name and last initial on a magnet; extra magnets for new students).
- Have the supplies and bookshelves organized and cabinets neatly labeled.
- Organize the desks in a double horseshoe arrangement, with my desk near the students' desks (extra desk(s), if possible).
- Attach the students' nametags to their desks. The nametags will also feature their numbers, which will be used throughout the year for homework

- purposes (extra blank nametags with numbers for new students).
- Have bellwork assignment on each desk with instructions for completion on the board.
- Have take-home folders with each student's name on the front prepared and inside each student's desk. On the inside, one pocket will say, "Homework," and the other pocket will say, "Stay-at-Home."
- Prepare the "All About Me" board by posting pictures and descriptions of my interests. (Use this board throughout the year to feature a "Student of the Week" with information supplied on an "All About Me" sheet.)
- Have procedures for arrival—getting the teacher's attention, getting students' attention, lining up, walking in the hallway, restroom, DEAR time, and dismissal posted—each done on paper with the same color background and border for easy recognition.
- Have rules posted on a different color than procedures; also have consequences and rewards for rules posted.
- Have "What do I do next?" sign posted in an easy-to-see location.
- Have student cubbies empty and labeled with their names and numbers (extra cubbies for new students).
- Have daily agenda posted on the board, each part and time of day on color coated laminated strips attached to the board with magnets and blank strips set aside for schedule changes.
- Have "Absent" and "Present" jar ready with all students' names on craft sticks inside the absent jar (to be moved to the present jar by students after procedure is explained).
- Have a jar of sharpened pencils ready.
- Have restroom cards prepared and hanging by the door.

Greeting Students

- Stand outside of the classroom next to the door and welcome each student with a smile.
- Ask for the ticket and verbally confirm that they are in the right classroom.
- Point out their personal number on the ticket and tell them to find their name or number on their desk and start their morning bellwork.

Teacher Welcome and Introduction

- Tell the students my name and use the "All About Me" board to share information.
- Tell the students that they will also get to share their information on the "All About Me" board later in the year.
- Express my high expectations for the year and how I look forward to teaching and learning with them.
- Pass out Bingo cards. Each square on the grid has a specific fun fact, such as "has two pets" or "loves pepperoni pizza." Explain that the students have ten minutes (set a timer) to find one classmate for each square who fits that square's criteria. The classmate must sign that square, and students may not have the same classmate sign twice on their Bingo cards.
- After the activity, discuss several of the fun facts that the students learned about their classmates.

First Seven Questions

There are seven essential questions students want answers to the moment they enter the classroom at the start of the school year.

1. Am I in the right room?
2. Where am I supposed to sit?
3. Who is my teacher as a person?
4. What are the rules of this classroom?
5. What will I be doing this year?
6. How will I be graded?
7. Will the teacher treat me fairly?

On the first day of school, **Oretha Ferguson** of Fort Smith, Arkansas, has a trifold that answers the seven questions plus more information on the organization of her high school classroom.

Cathy Terrell of Kansas answers the seven questions for her students with a PowerPoint presentation.

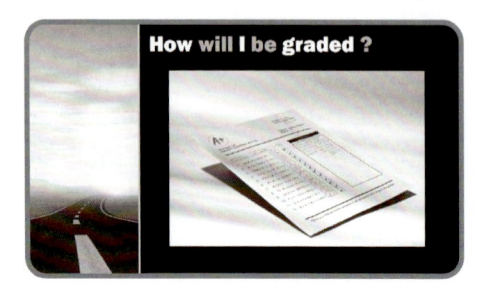

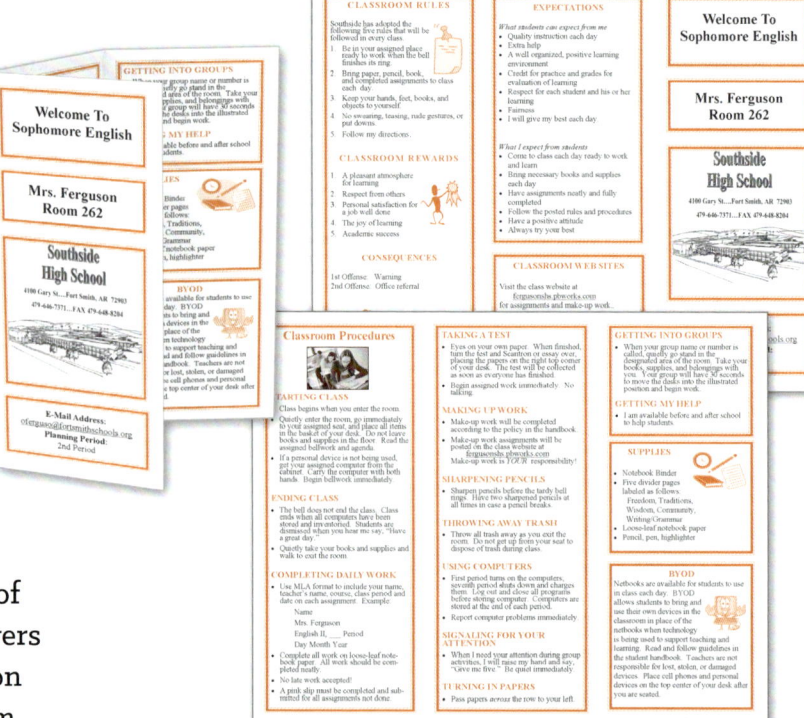

Classroom Procedures

Ms. Rogers
Room 332

Physical Science and Chemistry

Be Prepared!

The first day of teaching will be an exciting, anticipated event, but very daunting at the same time. You want teachers to feel in control of a complicated, challenging situation where they will encounter many individual needs and expectations.

High school teacher **Karen Rogers** of Kansas shares her expectations in a PowerPoint presentation on the first day of school.

Entering the Classroom
1. Pick up **handouts.**
2. Be **seated.**
3. Begin working on the **bellwork** assignment.

Daily Operation
1. Bellwork and attendance
2. Teacher information, instruction
3. Student work time

Dismissal
1. Clean up your area.
2. Be seated.
3. Push your chair in on the way out.

Classroom Rules
1. No defiance
2. No disruptions
3. No disrespect

Consequences
1. Verbal warning
2. Seat change
3. Remove from classroom
4. Call parents
5. Office referral

How to Get Good Grades
1. Attend class
2. Turn in assignments
3. Study for tests

Other Procedures
1. Visitors in classroom
2. Turning in assignments
3. Online learning
4. Room tour – student supplies, lab

Success in Science
1. Earn a science credit
2. Get good grades
3. Have fun
4. Thank you!

Safety Drills
Fire
1. Go out the door and turn right. →
2. Walk down stairs and out the door.
3. Stay together while teacher takes attendance.

Tornado
1. Go out the door and turn right. →
2. Walk down stairs to the bottom level.
3. Stay together while teacher takes attendance.

Lockdown
1. Teacher locks doors.
2. Stay calm, quiet, and out of sight until lockdown is over.

When students walk into the classroom, they want to feel that they are in capable hands.

Teachers are much more likely to create a consistent learning environment where students can flourish if they have put time and effort into planning and preparation.

After the hard work preparing for the first days of school, teachers will have the rest of the school year and the rest of their professional years ahead to truly enjoy life as a happy, content, successful, and effective teacher.

> **It is essential to have basic procedures ready for the first five minutes on the first day of school.**

Endnote

[1] Mona Alzahrani, Manal Alharbi, and Amani Alodwani, "The Effect of Social-Emotional Competence on Children Academic Achievement and Behavioral Development," *Canadian Center of Science and Education, International Education Studies* 12, no. 12 (November 29, 2019).

Induction Program Essentials

An induction program teaches effective classroom management and effective classroom instruction.

Teaching Successfully

> The purpose of an induction program is to immerse new teachers in a supportive collegial environment where they learn how to run a classroom successfully and how to effectively instruct students.

There is a reason you like to patronize certain businesses. It's because they are successful. These are the three characteristics of a successful business.

1. The business is well organized.
2. The merchandise or services are well delivered.
3. The customers are well treated.

Successful classrooms have the same three characteristics as a successful business.

1. The classroom is well organized.
2. The lessons are well delivered.
3. The students are well treated.

An effective induction program will initially focus on these two areas of training.

1. Classroom management—how the classroom is structured and organized so students can experience consistency
2. Instructional management—how lessons are taught so students know what to do to succeed

Induction Programs Teach Consistency

My students enjoy having a predictable classroom. They feel safe because they know what to expect each day. They like consistency in a world that can be very inconsistent.

Chelonnda Seroyer
Atlanta, Georgia

Teaching Effective Classroom Management

First things first. The very first thing a new teacher needs to learn is how to organize a classroom so it is well-run. When a classroom is well managed, discipline problems are minimized. A proactive approach to structure eliminates the possibility of classroom chaos and the need for a reactive response.

Effectiveness is not achieved with a haphazard approach. It is a methodical process to achieve success.

Following this notion, more teacher time can be dedicated to instruction and learning so that student learning time is maximized, and lessons are clearly presented.

Disordered, restless classrooms make teachers feel helpless and frustrated. They make students feel uncertain and apathetic.

It is imperative that during the induction process, teachers work together to develop practical classroom management plans. These plans are step-by-step guides on how to run a classroom in which instruction and learning can take place. **Procedures are the heart of a classroom management plan.** Procedures that become routines are the backbone of an efficient, organized classroom.

**The number one problem in the classroom is not discipline.
It is the lack of a classroom management plan with procedures and routines.**

Classroom management is the most misused term in education. Teachers who incorrectly define classroom management as discipline create a self-fulfilling prophecy that becomes the focus of their daily practice. Classroom management is about organization and consistency. Businesses are managed to be successful; the staff and clients are not disciplined to achieve success. **Effective, successful teachers manage a class; they don't discipline the class.**

There are significant differences between discipline plans and classroom management plans. Discipline plans have rules. Rules are explicit regulations that guide actions. If a rule is broken, there are negative consequences. Classroom management plans have procedures. Procedures are not rules. Procedures ensure students function in an acceptable and organized manner. A procedure is simply a method or process for getting things done in the classroom. If procedures are not followed, there are no consequences. The process is simply repeated correctly.

Teachers who view classroom management as a process of organizing and structuring classroom events tend to be much more effective than teachers who view their roles as disciplinarians.

> The most important system that is to be established at the start of school is consistency.
>
> In a culture of consistency, students will work, produce, learn, and achieve.

The Power of Procedures

Students do not like being in a classroom where they do not know what is going to happen next. They like consistency as it creates an environment that is safe and inviting, predictable and stable—where they can get on with learning.

Consistency frees up time to teach.

Many students come from home and living environments that are disorganized and inconsistent. Students want a plan. They want to know what to expect during their time at home.

The same is true of students in a classroom. Give them a well-managed, organized classroom with clear, daily practices and procedures, and they will respond positively. There are no perpetual admonishments, finger-pointing occurrences, or frustrating encounters reminding students what to do because they know what to do. They've been taught and rehearsed in the procedures of a classroom management plan. They know how the classroom and the lessons function.

> *I took over a classroom at the end of the first nine weeks, and it was a mess, physically and emotionally. I installed procedures and at the end of the school year the parents and students thanked me for putting a plan in place. The process works!*
>
> *No successful teacher can work without a classroom management plan.*
>
> Nick LaVecchia
> McKinney, Texas

No Problems and High Achievement

> *My classroom management plan is shared with my students on the first day of school, and I refer to this plan consistently. The students know what to do in the classroom, as well as how I expect them to act and to treat one another. They know how things work in our classroom because of the management plan and the procedures that are in place right at the beginning of the school year.*
>
> *I do not have any major behavior problems with my students. Most importantly, I always get high academic results from my students.*
>
> Sarah F. Jondahl
> Georgetown, Texas

> *For many of my at-risk students, this type of orderly and smoothly running classroom is the first experience of life without chaos.*
>
> **Stephanie Stoebe**
> **Round Rock, Texas**

Chapter 12: Induction Program Essentials • 99

Dear Students, See that blank space at the top of the paper . . . please write your name! Thank you!

Procedures lay the groundwork for student learning. As with everything else—be it playing a musical instrument, driving a car, or sports training—the more procedures are practiced, and the better they are learned, the faster they become routines. They become part of daily life in the classroom.

These are some typical and essential classroom procedures that should quickly become routines.

- Entering the classroom
- Putting away a backpack
- Beginning the opening assignment
- Asking for help
- Replacing a broken pencil
- Coming to attention
- Titling a paper
- Transitioning from task to task

> *I continue to be amazed at how much time and frustration I've wasted over the years trying to order my students to do what I want them to do instead of teaching them procedures so they know what they are responsible for.*
>
> Joel Hawbaker
> Rainbow City, Alabama

Procedures Produce Results

> *It occurred to me that McDonald's doesn't link their success to their ability to hire genius teenagers. What McDonald's has is a set of effective procedures that can get above average results from average teenagers.*
>
> *Now that's a plan.*
>
> Dr. Mike White
> Princeton City School District, Ohio

Students know what to do to start the day when procedures are part of the classroom culture.

100 • THE New Teacher Induction Book

Kayleen Randall is a librarian in Montana. She uses stuffed animals to illustrate and lead discussions on correct library procedures. Procedures are not just for the classroom. They are established throughout the campus. The school runs efficiently with an atmosphere of calm and focus that is created with procedures.

> *Procedures become routines. Procedures are what effective teachers do to help students become successful and engaged learners. Procedures help you be proactive and preventive, not reactive. It allows you to enjoy spending time with your students and getting to know them. Procedures give students structure, focus, guidance, and direction.*
>
> Laurie Jay
> Saskatoon, Canada

Induction Programs Teach Effective Instructional Management

The schools that achieve the best results are those with a clear idea of what kind of instructional practice they want to produce and then design a structure to go with it. **Alongside classroom management, instructional practice is the other essential component of an induction program.** The objective is to train teachers to have a clear instructional system in place so that they can continuously support their students as they strive toward successful academic performance.

According to the research of **Bruce Torff** at Hofstra University, the lack of classroom management and lesson-implementation skills is a bigger problem that the lack of content knowledge.[1]

The best instruction tells students what to learn and teachers what to teach. When both students and teachers are clear about what is to be learned, student learning is produced. This is known as "instructional clarity," or as **John Hattie** calls it, **Teacher Clarity**.[2]

Teacher clarity enhances student motivation and achievement and is one of the more positive influences on student success.

Influences with Positive Effects on Student Achievement[3]	
Influence	Effect Size
Teacher estimation	1.62
Collaborative impact	1.57
Self-reported grades	1.33
Teacher clarity	**0.75**
Reciprocal teaching	0.74
Feedback	0.70
Direct instruction	0.60
Spaced vs. massed practice	0.60
Mastery learning	0.57

When teachers are clear with their intentions, students are able to see the expectations for success.

Chapter 12: Induction Program Essentials • 101

Teacher clarity is very reassuring for students. There is no mystery about what learners are to achieve or what success looks like. Students do well when they are given explicit lesson objectives, leaving no room for confusion or doubt. They know how the instruction is organized and how they will be assessed and evaluated. It motivates them because they know exactly what to do to succeed.

The Learning Triangle

When lessons are clearly organized, there will be a result of 25 to 30 percent improvement in student performance or nine months of progress—a result every teacher, student, parent, and administrator wants.[4]

The Learning Triangle is the basis for organizing effective instruction. The concept of The Learning Triangle is used to create a consistent and stable lesson, a lesson that has clarity. There are three points to the learning triangle.

- **Objectives**—What students are to learn and what the teacher is to teach
- **Assessment**—What progress the learner is making
- **Instruction**—What are the best influences the teacher can use to teach

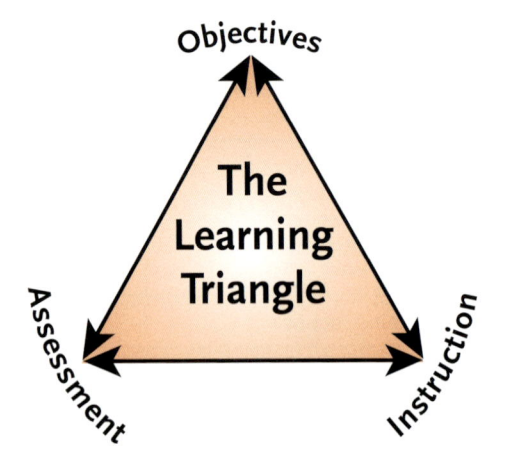

There is constant flow between the points on the triangle as each point influences the other two points.[5]

In an organized classroom that is consistent, students know
- what to **DO** (procedures), and
- what to **LEARN** (objectives).

In an organized classroom that is consistent, the teacher knows
- what to **TEACH** (instruction), and
- how to determine **PROGRESS** (assessment).

Effective teachers explain to students how the lesson and instruction are organized. Effective teachers teach well because they are clearly focused on what they want students to accomplish.

Organizing Instruction

An effective lesson plan has three basic, but essential components.[6]

1. **I do.** The teacher instructs using various strategies to achieve a goal.
2. **We do.** The teacher oversees engagement and practice by the class with feedback and assesses if the instruction has been effective. Tools are shared with students to self-assess their level of understanding.
3. **You do.** The student independently completes a task demonstrating learning of the goal.

These three elements are incorporated in the lesson planning process before implementation.

When teachers engage in instructional clarity, they assist and support students and give them every opportunity to succeed. When it comes to improving student achievement, all the research agrees on one very important finding—**what is taught and what is tested must be in alignment with the objective of the instruction.**

Essential Parts of an Effective Lesson

Objective **I do.**	Post the objective of the lesson so students will see what they are to learn.
Explanation **I do.**	Provide information, demonstrate, give examples, and a "grabber" to interest students in the lesson. Ideally, provide a link between prior knowledge and the new objective.
Guided Practice **We do.**	Display a problem or task so students see what they are to work on.
Check for Understanding **We do.**	Provide self-assessment techniques to provide immediate feedback to assist in understanding and learning. (See *THE Classroom Instruction Book*, chapters 10 and 11.)
Independent Practice **You do.**	Provide several other problems for students to work on individually or in groups. Students are to summarize the learning.
Evaluation **You do.**	Create and give a criterion-referenced test that is correlated to the objectives of the lesson.

Students Know How to Learn

Teacher clarity not only helps students learn, it teaches students **how to learn** and gives them the wherewithal to use what they have learned.

Chelonnda Seroyer, a high school teacher, has a highly organized lesson plan that is coherent, transparent, and clearly explained to her students.

There is no secret as to what is expected of my students. They all succeed because there is clarity about what they are to accomplish. When I do this, they have control over their success.

- **Objectives.** Clear and specific objectives are posted or provided—they know **where they are going**.
- **Guided Practice.** Students practice or do the assignment on what they are to learn—they know **what they are doing**.
- **Feedback.** Feedback is given to help students make progress—they know **how well they are doing**.
- **Assessment.** Instruction is adjusted based on assessment—students know **where to go next**.
- **Evaluation.** Students succeed because the evaluation is based on the lesson objectives—they know **how they will be tested** and have high expectations for a successful outcome.

Help Develop Teacher Impact

It cannot be said often enough—Teachers are a school's greatest asset. The more schools and districts invest in building the capacity of teachers through induction programs and professional development, the more expert they will be as classroom and instructional managers.

The path to teacher effectiveness is known and has been validated with extensive research. Share the continuum on page 106 with teachers so they can self-access with **The Effective Teacher Rubric** and chart their growth in proficiency.

An induction program is an opportunity to create teachers who have the capacity to positively affect student learning and achievement and at the same time be in control of their own future.

There are other benefits to an induction program.

- Induction programs familiarize teachers with the responsibilities, missions, and liaison philosophies of their districts and schools.

- Induction programs model how to collaborate professionally with colleagues.

One of the strongest influences on student achievement occurs when teachers work together and purposefully focus on instruction that will make an impact. **This is called Collaborative Impact and has an effect size of 1.57.**[7]

Influences with Positive Effects[8]	Effect Size
Teacher estimation	1.62
Collaborative impact	**1.57**

When teachers work together, they produce the highest results in student learning and achievement.

As administrators, coaches, education leaders, it is your responsibility to grow and nourish new teachers and induct them into a profession that offers support and sustenance for a strong and meaningful career.

Induction programs give teachers the practical knowledge and skills they need to run organized classrooms and implement lessons to ensure student success.

Care and nurturing in the beginning builds a strong and mighty future.

Clear Expectations for Success

Amanda Bivens knows that students will do well when she is transparent and clear about the expectations for their success. Her students know the lessons have been carefully constructed for them to succeed. She shares with the students her plan for their success in a straightforward, concise manner.

- *I will post a lesson objective so we both know what you are to learn.*
- *I will give you some background information to get you started.*
- *We will do a series of activities (lecture, video, labs, field trips, discussions, etc.) that will give you hands-on knowledge for the objectives.*

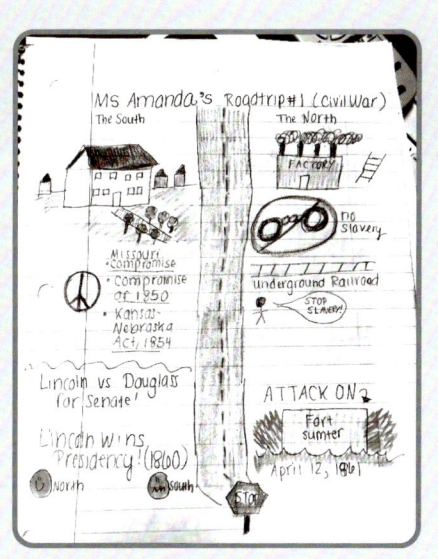

Assessing for understanding can be demonstrated in unlimited ways.

- *While you are working, I will check on your learning to help you make progress, sometimes telling you how to do something better, or just make suggestions.*
- *I will have you work in groups or teams because when you enter the adult workforce, your success will be in how well you can work and contribute to a group.*
- *I will next have you work alone to practice what you have learned to internalize it. Then, I want you to create, invent, and synthesize a product to demonstrate that you can do something with what you have learned.*
- *And don't worry about the test, as every test question will be correlated, sequenced, and structured to the lesson objectives.*

Chapter 12: Induction Program Essentials • 105

Continuum for Impact

How will your new teachers know if they are effective? Give them a means to self-assess their growth and development on the research-based, three characteristics of an effective teacher.

1. Classroom Management
2. Lesson Mastery
3. Positive Expectations

Self-assessment is not about evaluation; it is about self-improvement and realizing potential. This rubric is based on more than sixty years of research and will help teachers make progress towards their own professional growth to produce better student learning and have an impact on student achievement.

The Effective Teacher Rubric[9]

Topic / Effect	Mastery and Highly Effective	Proficient and Effective	Partially Effective	Needs Coaching
Classroom Management	Your students are responsible and know what to do so there is maximum engagement in all classroom activities.	You have a classroom management plan with procedures that structure the classroom.	You have some semblance of organization and structure in the classroom.	You have no classroom management plan, and the students have no idea what they are responsible for doing.
Lesson Mastery	You know how to instruct for teacher clarity, and your students know what is expected of them.	You know how to teach to objectives and use assessment tools to help students make progress.	You have an agenda with lesson objectives posted and teach to the objectives.	You just cover materials, do incoherent activities, and there is minimal work being done by the students.
Positive Expectations	You have created a consistent classroom culture where all students can learn and will succeed.	Your students have a sense of care and belonging and can see that you foster positive expectations for their success.	You have some consistency, but students aren't sure from day to day what is going to happen in the classroom.	Your classroom lacks consistency, and the students feel you don't care about them or their learning.

Endnotes

[1] Bruce Torff, "Getting It Wrong on Threats to Teaching Quality," *Phi Delta Kappan* 87, no. 4 (December 2005): 302–305.

[2] John Hattie, *Visible Learning: A Synthesis of Over 800 Meta-Analyses Relating to Achievement* (New York: Routledge, 2009).

[3] "Hattie Ranking: 256 Influences and Effect Sizes Related to Student Achievement," *Visible Learning*, accessed July 1, 2023, https://visible-learning.org/backup-hattie-ranking-256-effects-2017/.

[4] Hattie, *Visible Learning*.

[5] Harry Wong and Rosemary Wong, *THE Classroom Instruction Book* (Mountain View, CA: Harry K. Wong Publications, 2022).

[6] Wong and Wong, *THE Classroom Instruction Book*.

[7] Hattie, *Visible Learning*.

[8] *Visible Learning*, "Hattie Ranking: 256 Influences."

[9] "The Effective Teacher Rubric" was created by Harry and Rosemary Wong. Download a copy for personal, professional growth. To request permission to use outside of your school or district, please contact Harry or Rosemary Wong at RWong@HarryWong.com. https://www.EffectiveTeaching.com/TheEffectiveTeacherRubric.pdf

13 Recruiting New Teachers

The best induction programs teach new teachers how to deliver instruction with a clear understanding of what students need to learn.

Playing on a Winning Team

There is nothing better than playing on a winning team.

Isn't it obvious? If you are an actor, you want to perform in the best company. If you are in sports, there is nothing better than playing on a winning team. If you are a chef, you want to cook in a renowned restaurant. If you are an employee, you want to thrive in the best workplace. No one wants to be part of an unsuccessful enterprise.

It's the same in teaching. Sell your district or school as a place where new teachers will flourish and grow. In your employment, new teachers will
- be part of a two- to three-year induction program designed to help them become successful and effective teachers,
- be united with other teachers where they can cooperatively design lessons for student success, and
- have administrative support, encouragement, and validation.

The Supply and Demand of Teachers

The best way to recruit new teachers is to sell your district as a place where you will help them succeed.

There is a shortage of teachers, to reach more than 200,000 by 2025. It is a buyer's market and if you put your best foot forward, prospective teachers will respond.

Supply and Demand of Teachers[1]

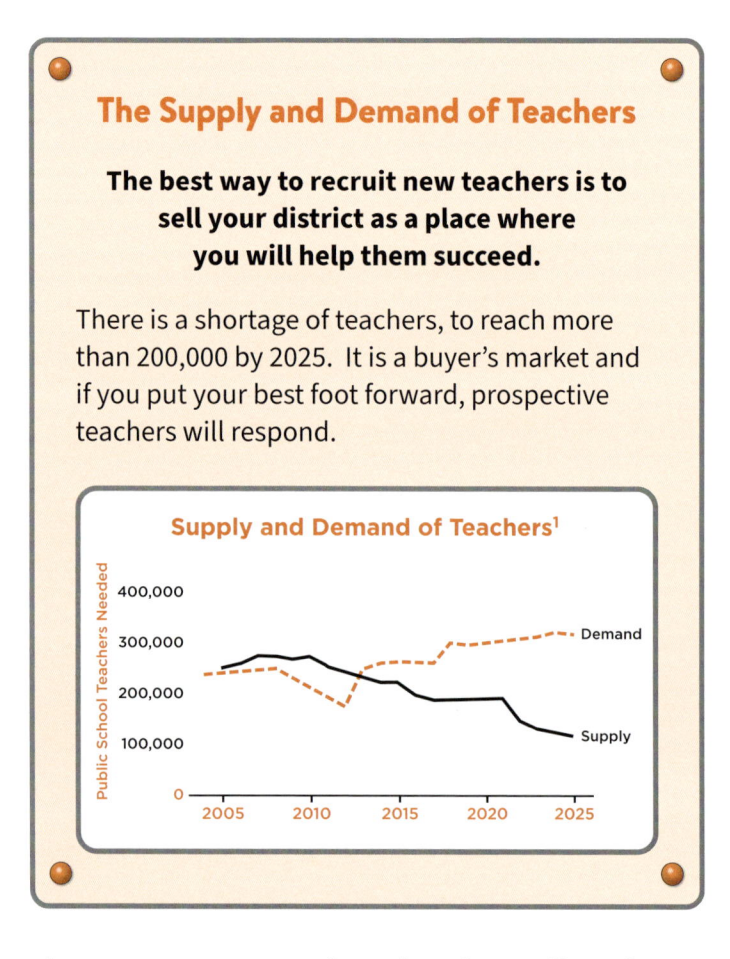

Show prospective teachers that they will not be alone. You are organized to help them succeed.

New teachers want a district that has a program that will teach them how to be an effective teacher. They want a district that has a program that will partner them with other effective teachers. They know if they are not effective, the students will devour them. They will leave stressed every day and depart within a year of what they dreamed of being—a teacher who has an impact on students and makes a difference in the world.

New teachers want to work for a district where **"the focus is on the students."** They do not want to work for a district where the focus is on a program or technology or is only interested in hiring another warm body to fill a vacancy, such as "we need someone to teach fifth grade." They can determine if a district is **"focused on the student"** if the district has a New Teacher Induction Program that is **"focused on building teacher capacity."**

> "Focused on the Students"
> is not the same as
> "Student or Child-centered"
>
> **Student-centered =
> Students determine** what they want
> to learn at their own pace.
>
> **Focused on the Students =
> Teachers determine** what and how
> the students will learn.

New teachers want to work in a district that has a clear understanding of what they can do to effect student learning. For this, there must be a curriculum that they can successfully follow. The primary reason teachers flee a school typically has nothing to do with the students, it's the lack of an academic culture. **Teachers seek schools where they can be successful.**

The Two Most Important Things

Just as most every company trains its new employees upon hiring, an effective school district has a **New Teacher Induction Program** that teaches the two most basic things needed to succeed as a teacher.

1. Classroom Management
2. Instructional Management

Selling Your School

When interviewing a prospective teacher, be cautious of how your school district is described. Is there an atmosphere where teachers are hired to implement a set program or is the culture one of building that teacher's teaching capacity?

Most often the principal is the major determiner as to who gets hired. If you are asked by the prospective teacher about your instructional program, how will you respond?

1. *Our staff is constantly reviewing our curriculum, and you are encouraged to be part of designing the curriculum for better student learning.*

2. *We have a really good program here at the school, and you will not want to do anything else besides the program we are already using.*

Teaching and learning are fluid, ongoing processes. Look for candidates who want to collaborate and be a part of continuous improvement. That is the teacher to hire—one to implement an instructional program that leads to student learning.

Chapter 13: Recruiting New Teachers • 109

1. <u>**Classroom Management**</u>:
   <u>How to organize and run the classroom</u>

When interviewing potential teachers, explain that the New Teacher Induction Program will teach the procedures used to run a successful classroom.

Watch students in a well-managed classroom and how they function.

- They are responsible for their time.
- They know and follow the procedures that structure the organization of the class.
- They are engaged and working.
- They are learning, achieving, and producing visible results.

Effective teachers have invisible procedures. You don't see them because the students have learned them. They have become routines—processes that happen automatically without prompts or thought. Classrooms that have procedures and routines in place run smoothly so that teaching and learning can take place in a safe and nurtured environment.

A student going to a school in an at-risk area said, "I like coming to this school, because everyone knows what to do. No one yells and screams at us, and we can get on with learning."

A teacher teaching in a vulnerable school said, "I like teaching in this school, because my students

He Said One Word

I visit eight schools in my role as an instructional coach.

One day I complimented the principal of one of them (a middle school) on the orderliness of the school, but more importantly, on the sense of responsibility his students exhibited and the respect they exhibited for each other, the teachers, and the property.

They always seemed to know exactly what to do and how to behave and there was nothing coercive about any of it. I observed one day how a teacher sent two students, unattended, into the library to make up a test. The librarian wasn't there yet, and the teacher had no idea I was present. The kids came in by themselves, took seats at tables far apart, and sat down facing the same direction. When each finished, they picked up their test and returned to the classroom—separately.

Kids constantly come into the library, without passes, just on trust. They checked out books without dilly-dallying and without loud talk—and then they returned to their classrooms. I sometimes leave my purse, my camera, my computer just sitting there on a library desk when I leave to visit a classroom. Never a worry.

So, I had much to compliment the principal on. I asked him "how he did it."

He turned to me and said one word, "Procedures."

**Sarah Powley
Tippecanoe, Indiana**

all know what to do. As a result, we can get on with learning."

> **Organization yields a lengthy career.**

Teachers who learn how to develop and implement a classroom management plan are more likely to enjoy long, meaningful careers in education.

> **With a plan ready in place, learning can begin. With learning comes achievement, and when achievement occurs, success for both teachers and students is sure to follow.**

An effective New Teacher Induction Program teaches effective classroom management skills.

2. <u>Instructional Management:
   How to teach the content so students learn and succeed</u>

When interviewing prospective teachers, share the curriculum for the grade level or subject that will be taught. The foundational element for teachers to teach effectively is a coherent, **content-rich curriculum.** Novice teachers, especially, must have an obvious curriculum to follow and teach to.

> **Teaching new teachers how to teach the curriculum is the core task of a New Teacher Induction Program.**

" They Beg Me to Test Them

When I begin each new lesson, I decide exactly what it is I want my students to know or be able to do. Then I tell or post my objectives so my students know what they will be learning and how they will show me they have learned it.

Next, I show them how to do it (instruction). We practice together (guided practice). Then they practice, even create things on their own (independent practice).

And then I test them the same way we practiced. In other words, how they will be tested. This way we all know exactly what we are learning and how we will know when and if we have learned it.

In my class, test is not a bad word. It is something my students look forward to. It is their chance to show me what they have learned. They can't wait for their turn to be tested because after all the instruction and practice, the test is the easiest part, at least that's what my students tell me.

They beg me to test them. They even stand in line waiting for their turn to show me what they have learned.

**Julie Johnson
Minnesota**

She Was Hired After Her First Job Interview

Jessica Ferguson, after graduating with a teaching degree, went to her first job interview. She walked in with a folder that contained her Classroom Management Plan. When asked what her strength was, she replied, "Classroom management. Here is a copy of my plan if you would like to review it. I will be happy to answer any questions."

She nailed the interview. The director of human resources called her six hours later to offer her a job. Why? She had a plan.

Jessica had her first day of school planned and ready before school was to begin.

You don't put together a recipe *after* you start cooking.

Preparation is the key to a successful outcome.

The purpose of instruction is to help people learn. The goal of a teacher is to expedite instruction to make learning easier, quicker, and more enjoyable. A teacher's job is to help everyone learn and be successful. Education should always be about student learning. **Students learn from instruction that is effectively provided.**

> **Teachers who are trained to use effective instructional techniques matter more to student achievement than any other aspect of schooling.**[2]

Teacher clarity (Chapter 12) in instruction provides the blueprint for successful outcomes. Students know the intention of the teaching with the success criteria for achieving the goal. When this formula for learning is used for instruction, instructional consistency is achieved.

A consistent instructional plan allows the curriculum to be taught with a highly probable success rate.

High-performing educational systems are successful because they have created instruction that is built around sound lesson plans. In Singapore, Finland, and Japan, instruction is understandable, transparent, and consistent. As such, progress, improvement, and sustainability are fostered each year as teachers thrive and students excel in a cohesive system.

An effective New Teacher Induction Program teaches effective instructional skills. (See Chapter 12 on The Learning Triangle to teach effective instructional skills.)

Collaborative Impact

High-performing school systems all have one characteristic in common. Their teachers all work together and demonstrate collaborative impact in their classrooms and professional lives.

The teachers being hired today come from a social world. **During the interview process, show how your district will**
- create a sense of belonging,
- bring teachers together to work collaboratively, and
- have a common curriculum for instructional success.

Impress the prospective teacher with an induction program that says good teachers make the difference. And that the district will provide structured, sustained induction, training, and support for their teachers to achieve what every school district seeks to achieve—improved student learning through improved professional learning.

Professionals do not work alone; they work in teams. When teachers meet in teams to focus on a problem, they become part of a team that will work to support students who need their help. Effective schools are committed to delivering learning. They are committed to imparting the necessary knowledge and competencies for students to thrive and succeed at school and in life.

In effective schools, teachers are part of a community of equals. They harness the collective intelligence, creativity, and genius of their teachers in consistent teams. They share common goals and aspirations.

Your school district will either hire another individual to fill a void, do little if anything to train that person and risk losing that teacher at the end of the school year or hire teachers with a commitment to provide them with a sustained, organized program for professional growth and continuous success.

> *The greatest crime in the world is not developing your potential. When you do what you do best, you are not only helping yourself, but the world.*
>
> **Roger Williams**

Endnotes

[1] Greg Wiggan, Delphia Smith, and Marcia Watson-Vandiver, "The National Teacher Shortage, Urban Education and the Cognitive Sociology of Labor," *The Urban Review* (2021).

[2] Holly Holland, "Teaching Teachers: Professional Development to Improve Student Achievement," *American Educational Research Association* 3, no. 1 (Summer 2005): 1–4.

14 How to Start and Sustain an Induction Program

An effective induction program is attainable and sustainable.

Select from Within

The resources to start an induction program are within your reach. Identify an effective teacher from your staff with a track record of student achievement. Tap that teacher to lead the program. There is no one better than another teacher who knows and understands what a new teacher needs.

Over thirty years ago, the superintendent of the Flowing Wells Unified School District (Chapter 6), tapped a teacher, **Susie Heintz**, and appointed her to design, orchestrate, and monitor a new teacher induction program. That program thrives to this day.

Susie Heintz

In 2008, **Gena McCluskey**, a then assistant superintendent and subsequent superintendent in Moberly, Missouri, tapped a middle school teacher, **Tara Link**, to start a new teacher induction program

Attaining and Sustaining

"If you want something you've never had, you must be willing to do something you've never done.

— Thomas Jefferson

1. Stop hesitating
2. Create a strong culture that others will want to join and be a part of
3. Balance the excitement of your program with the practicality and usability of its core components
4. Explore what others have done in induction programs to guide your development
5. Expect setbacks, but be elastic in your thinking
6. Gather a collection of future induction leaders from within the program
7. Build in metrics to measure desired outcomes
8. Celebrate successes
9. Repeat year after year after year

114 • THE New Teacher Induction Book

which she called S.H.I.N.E—Supporting, Helping, and Inspiring New Educators (Chapter 5). That program thrives to this day.

Gena McCluskey's motivation in starting an induction program stemmed from seeing that every building was starting over again each year. Schools were in a state of limbo—never making any progress in teacher development or student outcomes. She knew she had to find a way to create a system of support and professional development for the newly hired classroom teachers when they joined a staff.

The solution was obvious.

Training had to focus on the fundamentals of effective teaching and that became the basis of the Moberly induction program.

In the infinite wisdom of the Dyer County Tennessee school administrators, they appointed a teacher, **Amanda Bivens**, to coach the grade 3–5 teachers. As of 2022–2023 she has coached fifty-four teachers, and ALL are still in teaching. There has been no attrition under her coaching. She is a one-person induction program for her group of teachers that is still thriving to this day.

Empower an effective teacher to lead the way with a copy of this book as a resource and your induction program will thrive.

High-Performing Countries

High-performing countries possess a commonality. These countries train and empower their teachers to use their knowledge and skill.

- Teachers are trained in
  - their content area,
  - pedagogical skills, and
  - research procedures.
- Teachers have a cultural affinity and professional obligation to work together in collegial groups.

After training, teachers and principals are empowered to deliver the best possible instruction for every student.

Seems like a commonsense solution to an ever present problem in education—the lack of adequately trained teachers. And those countries with these practices achieve solid results and success with retention of teachers and student achievement scores.

> *Leadership and learning are indispensable to each other.*
> **John F. Kennedy**

Share Your Success

The programs shared in this book are led by educators who are eager to share their story and their success with you. If you start or have a sustainable induction program, please share the details with us so we can inspire, share, and help others. Please send the details to HWong@HarryWong.com. Thank you!

Lack of Sustainability

In the United States, no one talks about the curriculum, what teachers are to teach and what students are to learn. The relevant talk is about the latest program, technique, or technology.

For most school districts, there is no sustainable curriculum to focus on as a teaching collaborative.

Lack of direction leads to frustration and loss of vision.

There is no collective professional endeavor. There is no stewardship of a viable and transparent future.

The United States educational system is run on the endless, repetitive, futile cycle of chasing the silver bullet. We keep recycling unsuccessful programs giving them a new name and discarding them when something rousing comes along. This is similar to people who think nothing of throwing bait jars, cans, and trash overboard into lakes with no regard to the sustainability of the environment.

· Museum of Education Fads Gone By ·

A partial list of fads is on page 9, while the entire list of fads is in THE Classroom Instruction Book on page 267. It fills a page!

And into this swirling milieu, we throw newly hired teachers and expect them to succeed.

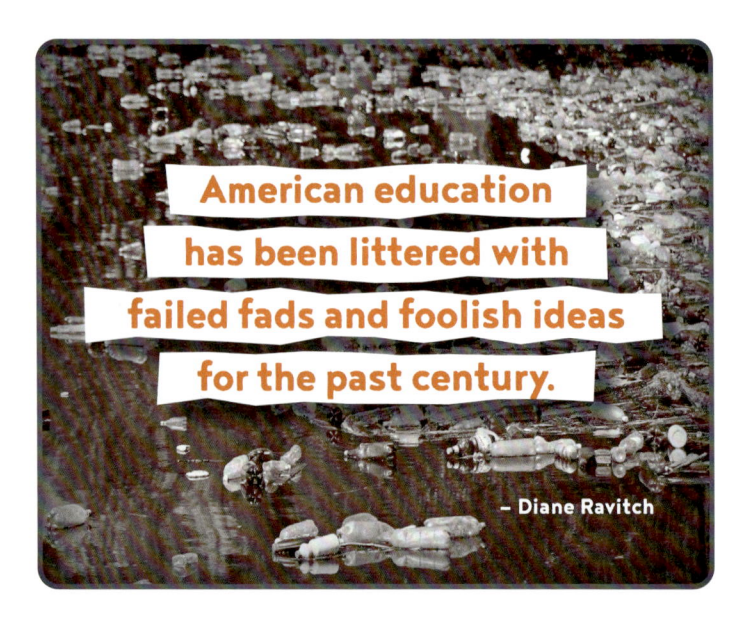

American education has been littered with failed fads and foolish ideas for the past century.

— Diane Ravitch

How to Solve the Problem

"We cannot solve our problems with the same thinking we used to create them.

Albert Einstein

The present and future crisis of teacher shortages is easily solved.

We must recruit and hire new teachers and then train them to retain them.

Teacher attrition costs the United States up to $2.2 billion annually. School districts must have systems in place to encourage and **recruit** the right candidates to become teachers.

Newly hired teachers must be **trained** in an organized and structured induction program to perform as highly effective teachers.

Teachers must be **retained**. Roughly half a million teachers either move or leave the profession out of frustration and lack of support.

116 • THE New Teacher Induction Book

Creating Sustainability

Sustainability means keeping a business running successfully with a viable and transparent future. It requires a willingness to set attainable goals and provide the path to reach them. It takes a leader who recognizes the value of creating a system of growth, collaboration, and belonging—where everyone shares in the toil and joy of teacher and student success. It's like the grower who tills and fertilizes the soil after each crop to get it into even better shape for the next planting.

To create a sustainable future, think outside of the box and cross territorial lines for viable ideas. Japan, Finland, and Singapore are three of the highest performing school systems in the world. They have achieved this status because their professional development program is sustainable. It begins with an induction process and then recurs day after day and year after year. (See Chapter 8.)

Incorporate these three components that are common in their programs into your sustainable induction program.

1. **Comprehensive structure.** The induction process is highly structured, rigorous, and seriously monitored. Induction leaders—staff developers, administrators, instructors, and coaches—have well-defined roles.

2. **Professional learning.** The meat of the program focuses on professional learning to deliver skills, growth, and expertise to teachers. The core components—classroom management and instruction—are delivered during induction and continue throughout a teacher's career. Good teaching is fostered throughout the school. **There is little difference between the strongest and weakest teachers.**

> ### Let's Do Lunch
>
> "I organize lunch dates with veteran teachers and teachers new to the school or new to the curriculum program. Over lunch they build a relationship and discuss teaching strategies or classroom management tips. Once the ice is broken, they themselves reach out and continue the relationship. The more experienced teachers then invite the new teachers to their classrooms for observations.
>
> This speeds up the process of settling in and finding friends on the staff.
>
> Rima Singh
> Gurgaon, India

3. **Collaboration. Collaboration is the forte of sustainable growth and performance.** Collaborative group work is understood, fostered, and accepted as part of the teaching culture. **Teachers are never abandoned in their classrooms.** There are shared experiences, shared practices, shared tools, and a shared language among all colleagues. And it is the function of the induction phase to engender this sense of group identity and treat new teachers as colleagues and cohorts.

Practicing Collaboration

<u>Japan:</u> The teachers' room has been in existence for 140 years and is an integral part of a teacher's life. Teacher preparation takes place inside of this collaborative, social space. In this area, overseen by administrators, all teachers have individual desks and meet daily to prepare, complete work, and collaborate on practice. It is a place to bounce ideas while having a cup of tea.

SUSTAINABILITY

"DO WELL" — Implement Induction Program

"DO GOOD" — Retain Effective Teachers

Because everyone knows what to do, they can teach a new teacher what to do.

New teachers are tutored by their colleagues and administrators, the very same people with whom they will be working. The veteran teachers want a new teacher to be up-to-speed as quickly as possible because they are part of their team. As a new teacher, it's very reassuring to know you're working with people who know what they are doing, and they are eager to teach you how to do things, too. **Effective teaching is transferred to new teachers and sustained day after day and year after year.**

A new teacher is introduced to the teachers' room the first day of employment. The teachers' room tells the new teachers that they belong and have access to their more experienced colleagues and can have substantial and ongoing communication and support. **The new teacher becomes part of a sustainable system.**

When everyone gathers in the teachers' room, teachers can support their common purpose regardless of their years of experience. Everyone learns together. The ongoing and unplanned nature of learning that takes place is critical to a teacher's professional growth.

> In Japanese schools, the teachers' room is an invaluable place for teachers to learn together over their careers.

No one teaches alone in Japan. You are made welcome and feel you belong on your first day as a teacher.

Is there an existing space in your school that is no longer in use that can be transformed into a teachers' room?

Finland: From the minute a new teacher joins a staff in Finland, they are immersed in teamwork, working with colleagues to create lessons, improve instruction, and assess outcomes. Teaching and learning are joint responsibilities that are rooted in the professional culture of Finland's teachers. Meetings are part of the teacher's assignment. Everyone works together to elevate learning.

Groups of teachers visit each other's classrooms and plan lessons together in a system that includes sharing resources and knowledge.

You are part of collegial networks for professional growth.

Finland trusts its teachers because they know their teachers know what they are doing. When collaboration is the culture and trust is the bedrock, the system is sustainable.

Singapore: Singapore's prevailing culture is that collaborative sharing is ubiquitous and consistent. There is a common room where all belong. In the common room new teachers can ask pressing questions, share immediate concerns, and ask for help without fear of being judged. Rapport and camaraderie are developed among teachers through both formal meetings and informal daily interaction. Assistance is just a desk away. Teachers help one another with lesson plans, materials preparation, test questions, and even classroom management.

The synergy created out of this shared experience allows teachers to continually grow as educators, departments to coordinate their curriculums, and for more experienced teachers to pass on their knowledge to newer teachers.

With a common room, novice teachers will find the entire staff is there to support and help them learn to be successful the second they start as new teachers with assigned senior teacher-coaches. In addition, the new teacher will also have a buddy-coach in the same subject or in the same department to navigate the ins and outs of teaching. New teachers are observed and tutored by grade-level chairs, subject-area chairs, and department heads. Everyone aspires to help new teachers adjust, improve, and perform.

The common room is a common space where the minds meet and relationships form, where every teacher in the school is working towards the common goal of helping each other and growing in the process.

When teachers in Singapore talk to each other, they have a common language. There is an installed culture. Everyone is on the same page. There is a shared pedagogical understanding. They know how to teach the curriculum for mastery.

Singaporean teachers can explain their curriculum and then describe the instructional process of how it is implemented. They know what aspects are needed to be an effective teacher and they then train themselves for 100 hours each year until they retire. Learning and growth are ongoing.

> In its short history, Singapore has created a sustainable system that is the envy of the world.

There are no teacher shortages in countries with a sustainable professional development system. Everyone belongs and everyone stays.

Investing in Sustainable Induction Programs

Teachers are the number one reason for success or failure in the classroom. To keep good teachers, education leaders need to realize that people crave connection. Belonging, a basic human need, translates into keeping skilled teachers when structured, training programs are in place that prepare new teachers and renew veteran teachers for the rigor of the classroom. Induction programs provide that bridge because they are structured around a learning community of equals, where fresh ideas are valued and respected the same as practices that have been in place.

A successful and effective induction program
- treats every colleague as a potential valuable contributor,
- creates learning communities where everyone, new teachers as well as veteran teachers, gains knowledge, and
- demonstrates that quality teaching becomes not just an individual responsibility, but a group responsibility as well.

Teachers remain with a district when they feel supported by administrators, have strong bonds with their colleagues, and are collectively committed to pursuing a common vision for student learning in a performance-oriented culture as they grow in the profession. They want to stay in a district that sustains a culture of consistency in its practices.

Trained teachers are effective teachers.

New teachers are waiting to be welcomed on their journey of affecting lives.

> Districts and schools that provide structured, sustained training for its teachers achieve what every school district seeks to achieve—improved student learning.

The teachers hired today are the teachers for Generation Alpha. Their effectiveness will determine the success of multiple generations of students. Their effectiveness can be ensured by providing them with a comprehensive, coherent professional development program that begins with a **New Teacher Induction Program**.

Your effectiveness as a leader will be measured by your commitment and dedication to creating a culture where teaches will flourish and succeed and students will learn and grow. The profession is counting on you to lead. The future is counting on you to succeed.

> *Just Do It*
>
> **Nike**

Afterword

> *We can't keep preparing them, even if we change our preparation program, to be more flexible and accessible if we don't have schools to change to keep them. We've got to change schools. It's not okay that teachers sit in their cars crying in October.*[1]
>
> Carole Basile, Dean
> Arizona State University Teacher's College

When teachers end up in cars crying, give up in frustration, and leave the profession, it is not because they could not cut it. It is because the system that hired them failed them.

The role of an administrator is to hire and develop effective teachers. We lament the teacher shortage and the ability to find qualified teachers. Even the less-than-qualified teachers are leaving because of the lack of support.

This is an urgent call for you to be the agent of change for the teachers in your school, in your district. Don't succumb to the dysfunctional prevailing norm.

Be brave. Embrace the concept of induction and do it to the best of your ability. Even the first step is a step in the right direction and is better than doing nothing at all. Look to other programs for inspiration and guidance. It is OK not to know how, but be willing to grow and to learn along the way. Close your eyes and envision the teachers you want in your classrooms. Now chase that vision with ferocity and passion. Half-heartedness will yield halfhearted results. This will be a journey to be celebrated as milestones are reached.

We have classrooms full of students desperately in need of qualified, effective teachers. Put your next group of newly hired teachers through an induction program that focuses on effective classroom management and classroom instruction, and you can change the culture of your school and close the student achievement gap in just a few years. The impact will be visible and measurable.

We must begin to develop the world's most precious resource—its teachers. On average, teachers in the United States see 3,000 students in their career. And almost everyone agrees that a good teacher can change the course of a student's life.[2]

Build a future for your teachers with a New Teacher Induction Program that will create and sustain the quality of education offered at your school. Be the true leader for your teachers and your students. The future is in your hands.

---

[1] Marianna McMurdock, "Traditional University Teacher Ed Programs Face Enrollment Declines, Staff Cuts." September 22, 2022, https://www.the74million.org/article/traditional-university-teacher-ed-programs-face-enrollment-declines-staff-cuts/.

[2] Stacy Torino, "12 Powerful Statistics That Prove Why Teachers Matter," May 15, 2019, https://www.weareteachers.com/teacher-impact-statistics/.

About the Authors

Harry K. Wong and Rosemary T. Wong

Harry and Rosemary are new teacher advocates, motivational speakers, and inspirational leaders. Colleagues have described them as connectors, angels, gurus, encouragers, cheerleaders, and rock stars who are enthusiastic, down-to-earth, patient, kind, giving, and real.

They are the authors of *THE First Days of School*, a book that has sold more than 4.5 million copies and is available in ten languages. It is used in over 2000 college classes to train potential new teachers. Thousands of school districts use it in their professional development programs.

They are also the authors of *THE Classroom Management Book* and *THE Classroom Instruction Book*, written to create effective teachers who can produce student learning.

Their eLearning course, *THE Classroom Management Course*, has been used by districts to train teachers, especially those new to the profession, on how to create a classroom environment where learning will thrive.

Their materials have a solid foundation of research, are not controversial, and suggest practical techniques that are practical, enduring, and produce immediate results.

Their complete bios can be accessed at www.HarryWong.com.

Index

A

aboard, welcomed, 47
absent-from-class form, 87
academic growth of students, 5
Academy-based learning, 9
Academy of Singapore Teachers, 63
Academy, Walmart, 74
acceptance rate, lower, 61
Accomplished-based learning, 9
acculturate, 11–13
achievement, 3, 14–15, 23–24, 41, 55, 66, 101, 104, 107, 111
achievement and attendance, 55
Achievement-based assessment, 9
achievement gap, 10, 20
action, 13, 15, 61, 63, 69, 119
    community in, 47
    course of, 14
action research team, 10
activities, 21–23, 43, 50, 61, 93, 105
    guided practice, 90
    incoherent, 106
    in-service, 56
    sponge, 90
Adaptive assessment, 9
Adaptive learning, 9
Adaptive technology, 9
administrative committees, 64
administrative cost, 79–80
administrative support, 108
    little, 30
administrator positions, 79
administrators, 10, 17–18, 20–21, 31, 38–39, 43, 45, 55, 59, 64–65, 67, 69, 71, 80, 84, 102, 105, 115, 117–118, 120
administrators and high-performing teachers, 31
administrators and teachers volunteer, 68
after-school programs, 9
Afterword, 122
agenda, 18, 29–30, 92, 106
    daily, 90–91, 93
    posted, 91
alignment, 70, 102

Alignment of assessment, 9
All About Me, 93
Alliance for Excellent Education, 78
Alternative assessment, 9
American educational system, 7, 28, 116
annual loss, 77, 83
aptitude, 59, 61, 80
Argument Driven Inquiry, 9
Arizona, 45–46, 52
arrangements
    cooperative, 56
    special, 68
    travel, 80
Art-centered learning, 9
aspirations, 113
Asquith, Christina, 6
Assertive discipline, 9
assessment, 31, 63, 67, 102, 104, 111
    regular, 56
Assessment-based achievement, 9
assessment tools, 106
assets, 2–3, 10, 20, 41–43, 56, 67, 74, 104
    physical, 10
    valuable, 56
assignments, 55, 81, 87, 90–91, 104
    bellwork, 91–93
    committee, 56
    comprehension, 92
    missing, 92
    opening, 90–91, 100
    workbook, 73
    worst, 7
associates, 74
atmosphere, 38–39, 101, 109
at-risk schools, 83
attendance, 43, 55, 87, 91–92
attributes, critical, 45
attrition, 4, 37, 39, 41, 77–78, 84, 115
    little, 37
attrition rate, higher, 52
attrition rates, 7, 52
Audio Lingual Method, 9
average cost, 82–83
average salary, 79

B

Barth, Roland, 17
Basile, Carole, 122
Before Students Arrive Checklist, 92
Beginning Teacher Induction Program. *See* BTIP
beginning teachers, 6–7, 22, 83
beliefs, 16–17, 23, 33, 50, 63–64, 78
    core, 63
    shared, 23
bellwork, 47, 90, 93
Bivens, Amanda, 4, 77–78, 85, 105, 115
Blended learning, 9
Block scheduling, 9
blueprint, 112
bodies, warm, 81–82, 109, 113
bonds, strong, 18, 120
Brain compatibility, 9
BTIP (Beginning Teacher Induction Program), 39
buddy-coach, 63, 119
building principal, 42
building teacher capacity, 17, 19–20, 23, 39, 46, 59, 62, 64, 71, 76, 104, 109, 115
building trust, 63
businesses
    core, 11
    successful, 97
businesses train, 13, 72
business leaders, 10
buyer's market, 108

C

capabilities and performance of teachers, 8
capacity
    collective, 19
    developing teacher, 71
    human, 46
    improved, 51
    instructional, 32
    maximize, 59
    nation's, 41, 79
    potential intellectual, 77, 83
    professional, 69
    teacher's teaching, 109
capacity of teachers, 3, 20, 51, 59–60, 66–67, 71, 104
Care-based practices, 9
career ladder, 65
career path, 64
careers, 13, 23, 29, 39, 42, 45, 49, 53, 61–62, 64, 66, 69, 71, 74, 88, 105, 111, 118
caring, 9, 56
Case-based learning, 9
celebrate, 56, 114
celebration, end-of-year recognition, 43
Challenge-based learning, 9
Chandia, Shaunene, 38
checklist, 47, 56, 79, 89–90
    start of school, 89
Cheesecake Factory, The, 75
Chicago Public Schools, 83
children, 4, 7, 10, 16–17, 67, 91–93
China, 68, 70
citizens, senior, 75
clarity, instructional, 101–102
Clark County, 37, 39
class, 90–92, 98, 102, 110–111
    first, 88
    quiet, 90
class instruction, 59
classroom, 3, 5, 14, 31, 37, 39–40, 42–43, 47–48, 50, 56, 63, 74, 77–78, 81, 87–88, 90–93, 96–100, 104, 106, 110, 113, 117, 119
    best, 90
    consistent, 106
    demonstration, 20, 47–48

    effective, 82
    flipped, 8–9
    isolated, 30
    organized, 98–99, 102, 105
    prettiest, 78
    restless, 98
    right, 93
    visit, 61, 68
    well-managed, 90, 110
    well-structured, 14
    worst, 7
classroom behavior, 10
classroom chaos, 97
classroom environment, 50, 90
classroom experience, 30
    secondary model, 42
classroom instruction, effective, 97
Classroom Instruction Book, THE, 103, 116
classroom management, 1, 27, 29, 39, 42, 47, 78, 90, 97–98, 101, 109–10, 112, 117, 119, 122
Classroom Management Book, THE, 42
classroom management plan, 42, 92, 98–99, 106, 111–112
classroom management skills, 78
    effective, 111
classroom management strategies, 26, 43
classroom management tips, 47
classroom managers, 59
classroom procedures, 55
    essential, 100
class sizes, 10, 15, 19, 41, 59, 84
cleanliness, 66, 76
Clear Expectations for Success, 105
Clerestory Learning, 9
clients, toughest, 7
coaches, 4, 30–31, 43, 48, 64, 69, 77, 105, 115, 117
    behavior, 43
    great, 18
    instructional, 51
coaching, 3, 30–31, 43, 50, 59–60, 64, 75, 77, 106, 115
coaching groups, 56
cohorts, 43, 60, 69–70, 117
collaboration, 5–6, 15, 17–19, 22, 32, 43, 51, 61, 69, 117, 119

    culture of, 19, 39, 41, 65
    professional, 23
    school culture of, 41
collaborative culture, 15, 17, 19
collaborative Endeavor, 5, 15
collaborative group work, 69, 117
collaborative impact, 14–15, 17, 23, 31, 42–43, 101, 104, 113
    core feature, 23
collaborative impact on new teachers, 42
collaborative learning, 1, 63
collaborative mission, 13
collaborative teams, 18, 39
colleagues, 5, 16, 18, 21, 32, 39, 62–65, 68–70, 104, 117–118, 120
    experienced, 83, 118
    replacing, 81
collective efficacy, 14
collegial, 25, 29, 47, 119
commitment, 17, 19, 46, 53–54, 66, 69, 113
    school's, 53
    shared, 59, 69
    staff person's, 13
commitment to train, 113
commonalities, induction programs, 69, 115
common sense, 10
Communication Arts, 91
community, 23, 33, 42–43, 51, 56, 62, 113
    at-risk, 110
    cultural, 70
    professional, 20, 51
    unique, 45
Community-based learning, 9
community property, 68, 70
community resources, 42
companies, successful, 76
competencies, 75, 113
competencies for students, 113
components, 14, 21, 42, 69–70, 75, 117
    basic, 102
    core, 114, 117
    critical, 10
    essential, 101
comprehensive induction programs, 23, 49, 71

comprehensive structure, 69–70, 117
comprehensive training program, 75
Computer-based reading, 9
Concerns-based improvement, 9
Conley, Maureen, 91
connection, 5, 18, 26–27, 29, 31, 53, 120
   crave, 120
connect teaching effectiveness, 6, 61
consequences of mentoring, 27
consistency, 30, 41, 63, 90, 97–99, 106, 120
   instructional, 112
constructive feedback, 19
Constructivism, 9
content, 27, 96, 111
   mastery of, 78
content areas, 43, 48, 115
content, pedagogical knowledge, 61, 64
content-rich core curriculum, 67
continuity, 18, 41
continuous professional development, 45, 48–49, 59, 69, 71
Continuous Professional Development (CPD), 69
cooperation, 15, 19
cost of educating teachers, 81
cost of reducing class size, 84
cost of teacher attrition, 41, 78–82, 84–85
costs of recruiting, 82
countries, 6, 41, 61–62, 69, 71, 80, 115, 120
   high-performing, 6, 13, 20, 32, 45, 49, 59–60, 69, 71, 80, 115
   high-ranking, 15, 19
CPD. *See* Continuous Professional Development
credibility, 21
Culturally responsive teaching, 9
culture, 3, 6, 11, 13, 15, 17–18, 20, 22, 31, 38–39, 43, 45, 47, 50, 62–63, 82, 88, 98, 106, 109, 119–120
   academic, 109
   caring, 52

common, 20
installed, 119
performance-oriented, 120
pervasive, 70
positive, 39
strong, 32, 114
culture in Finland, 6
culture in Japan, 6
curriculum, 3–6, 8–9, 13, 21, 27, 38, 47, 59, 64, 69, 81, 109, 111–112, 115, 117, 119
   coherent, 7
   common, 113
   content-rich, 59, 71, 111
   effective, 61
   sustainable, 115
Curriculum-based measurements, 9
cycle
   chronic, 82
   futile, 8, 116

D

Darby, Jeanette, 12
Data driven instruction, 9
Dead Horses, 10
Deficit/Abundance Model, 9
demonstration classroom, 17
demonstration lessons, 66, 68
demonstration teaching, 50
department heads, 63–64, 71, 119
depleting school budgets, 85
Designated Trainer (DT), 75
Design-based learning, 9
desks, 5, 65, 92–93, 117, 119
Detracking, 9
development, professional, 26, 32, 45, 59–60, 67, 71, 114
development of teachers and students, 9
Diaz, Victor, 52
didacticians, 6, 26, 61, 70
difference, little, 67, 117
Differentiated instruction, 9, 15
Digital-based learning, 9
Direct instruction, 14, 101
disciplinarians, 98

discipline, 50, 63, 98
discipline and managing students, 50
discipline plans, 47, 98
discipline plans and classroom management plans, 98
discipline problems, 97
Discovery method, 9
district's culture, 13–14, 23
district's mission, 45, 47
district's staff development program, 46
district's training program, 45
district technology programs, 43
Diversity-based curriculum, 9
Domino's, 73–74, 76
Drucker, Peter, 10
Dual-enrollment program, 9
Dufour, Rick, 19
duties, troublesome non-teaching, 7
Dyer County School District, 4, 77, 115

E

Earth-bound education, 9
education, 3, 14–15, 19, 23–25, 27, 32, 34, 41, 43, 46, 57, 60–64, 67, 71, 78, 80, 83, 85, 96, 98, 111–112, 115
   high-quality early childhood, 41
   post-secondary, 62
   special, 41, 81
   teacher's, 87
education experts, 19
Education Fads, 116
education terms, 47
educator, great, 56
educators, 17, 33, 38, 61–63, 115, 119–120
   helping fellow, 38
Edwards, Jacinda, 92
effect
   negative, 19
   single greatest, 5
"Effect, The Widget," 32

effective instruction, 47, 82, 102
    developing, 17
effective instruction components, 42
effective lesson, 103
effective lesson plans, 68, 102
effectiveness, 3, 5, 13, 18, 20, 27, 41, 52, 62, 98, 120
    instructional, 10, 21, 67
effectiveness of mentoring, 27
effectiveness of stay interview, 52
effective practices, 31
    developing, 68
effective school administrators, 21
effective school districts, 31, 49, 51, 109
effective school year, 20
effective teacher gap, 15
"Effective Teacher Rubric, The," 106
effect of home environment, 15
effect of parental involvement, 15
effect of prior achievement, 15
effect on student achievement, 1, 3, 41
effect size, 14, 19, 101, 104, 107
effect student learning, 109
efficacy of mentoring, 28
Einstein, Albert, 116
Embodied learning, 9
Emotional intelligence, 9
emotional support, 31, 50
empirical scrutiny, 27
encouragement, positive, 42–43
Endnotes, 11, 24, 34, 40, 44, 57, 71, 85, 96, 107, 113
engagement, 53, 102
    instructional, 39
    maximum, 106
    teacher's, 52
environment
    academic, 14
    at-risk, 83
    living, 99
    nurtured, 110
    organized, 90
    supportive collegial, 97
equity, increasing, 68
evaluation, 6, 13, 49, 52–53, 61, 68, 103–104, 119
    negative, 27
Evans, Dennis, 83
Evidence-based education, 9

exit interview, 22, 52, 55, 79
expectations, 14, 33, 37–38, 43, 50, 95, 101, 105–106, 113
    district, 42
    high, 93, 104
    positive, 78, 88, 106
experience, 27–28, 30, 55, 60, 78, 87, 118
    collective, 19
    educational, 89
    first, 99
    initial, 82
    shared, 119
experienced teachers, 7, 38–39, 56, 117, 119
experience success, 15, 31, 120
Experiential education, 9
expert, 30, 49, 104
    subject matter, 75
expertise, 28, 69
expert teachers, 46, 49, 51

F

factors
    critical, 5, 21, 68
    meaningful, 10
    predominant, 10
fads, 7–9, 32, 63, 66, 115–116
    failed, 9, 116
    futility, 7
    makeshift, 59
fads believing, 78
fads-of-the-month, 15
Fantasy, 8
Farris, Elaine, 21
fast-food worker, 75
feedback, 14, 17, 21, 31, 49–50, 54–56, 63, 66, 83, 91, 101–104
Feiman-Nemser, Sharon, 27
Ferguson, Jessica, 112
Ferguson, Oretha, 94
Ferguson, Ronald, 33
Fifth Grade, 92
findings, important, 102
Finland, 5–6, 13, 26, 61–62, 65, 70, 80, 112, 117, 119
    collaboration in, 6

first, 3, 94, 97
first day, 3, 5–6, 12, 47–48, 65, 82, 87–90, 92, 94–96, 99, 112, 118
first day of employment, 118
first day of school
    Finland, 5
    Japan, 5
First Days of School, THE, 47, 50
First Five Minutes, 87, 90
First Grade, 91
first impressions, 73, 87
Flowing Wells Formalized Training Chart, 49
Flowing Wells Unified School District, 45–51, 114
formal hierarchy, 6
formation, systematic, 29
Four-day schools, 9
four day school week, 9
Friedman, Thomas, 19, 69
fulfillment, 39
fundamentals, 4, 115
furusiyya, 28

G

Game-based learning, 9
Games-based curriculum, 9
gaps, smallest, 69
Garden-based learning, 9
Garet, Michael, 22
Generation Alpha, 120
Gibbs, Joe, 10
Gill, Ayesha, 62
goals, 9, 13, 18, 20–21, 25–27, 29–31, 45, 47, 53, 56, 76, 92, 102, 112, 117
    articulated, 49
    common, 37–38, 113, 119
    personal, 52
Goals 2000, 9
Goodlad, John, 5
Good morning, 92
grabber, 103
Great Tragedy of Mentoring, 26
greeting students, 93
Gregory, Toby, 48
group identity, 69, 117

groups
- collaborative, 63
- collegial, 115, 119
- cooperative, 47, 65

growth, 56, 69, 104, 117, 119
- academic, 5
- personal, 74
- professional, 10, 22, 45, 49, 51, 107, 118
- sustainable, 117

guide-by-the-side, 25–26, 70
guided practice, 103–104, 111
Guskey, Thomas, 22

H

Haberman, Martin, 8
habit, positive, 66
Hackett, Brandy, 91
hallmark, 4, 18, 21, 87
Hamburger University, 75
Hanushek, Eric, 23
haphazard, 25, 29–30
happiness check-in, 52
Harvard Graduate School of Education, 60
Hattie, John, 14, 19, 101
Hawbaker, Joel, 100
Hearne, Joan, 23
Heintz, Susie, 46, 114
Helsinki University, 61
hemisphericity, 9
Hendricks, J. Robert, iii
high-capacity teaching workforce, 62
highest impact on student learning and achievement, 14, 104
High-leveraged content, 9
high-performing school systems, 21, 59, 65, 113
high-stakes testing, 9
high turnover rates, 41, 79, 83
homework, 55, 92–93
Huberman, Michael, 22
human capital, 4
Hybrid learning, 9

I

impact, 8, 10, 15, 18, 21–24, 28, 39, 55, 59, 65, 104, 108
implementing strategies, 84–85
improvement, continuous, 109
independent practice, 103, 111
individualized instruction, 19
induction, 1–2, 5–6, 12–14, 18, 22–23, 25, 27, 42, 47–50, 60–62, 65–72, 89, 117–118, 122
- sustained, 113

induction activities, 70
induction events, ongoing, 39
induction in Canada, 66–67, 70
induction in Finland, 61
induction in Japan, 65
induction in Shanghai, 68
induction in Singapore, 62
induction leader checklist, 56, 114, 117
induction process, 11, 14, 18, 30, 33, 38–39, 45, 60, 74, 84, 98, 117
induction program
- effective, 12–13, 20, 32, 97, 114, 120
- sustainable, 115, 117, 120

influences, 14–15, 23, 101–102, 104, 107
- highest, 14
- powerful, 15

Influences and Effect Sizes, 107
influences on student achievement, 15, 23, 104
in-house induction training program, 38
innovations, educational, 5
Inquiry-based learning, 9
Institute for Teacher Renewal and Growth, iii, 46, 49
instruction, 6, 8–9, 13, 15, 21, 38–39, 42–43, 47, 62, 64–66, 71–72, 75, 89, 91–93, 98, 102, 104, 108, 111–112
- best, 101
- effective components, 42

Instructional Coach, 4, 77–78, 110
instructional management, 97, 109, 111, 122
instructional managers, 104
instructional methods, 14
instructional plan, consistent, 112
instructional practices, 21, 47, 51, 101
- effective, 45, 47, 51

instructional strategies, 48, 50
- evidence-based, 17

instructional techniques, 13, 29
interaction, positive, 52
Interdisciplinary teaching, 9
interviewing prospective teacher, 109
isolation, 3, 5–7, 13, 15, 17–18, 25, 31, 40, 42, 61, 70

J

Jackson, Phil, 18
Japan, 5, 26, 117
- collaboration in, 6

Jay, Laurie, 101
Jefferson, Thomas, 114
job-embedded induction, 31
job interview, first, 112
job-satisfaction ratings, highest, 73
Johnson, Julie, 111
Jondahl, Sarah F., 92, 99
Jones, Emily, 78
journey, professional, 48, 54

K

Katie's classroom, 16–17
Kennedy, John F., 115
key to lifelong success, 15
key word in mentoring, 30
Korea, 80
Kraft, Matthew, 55

L

Land-based learning, 9
language, common, 17, 43, 63, 69, 117, 119
LaVecchia, Nick, 99
leadership, 21, 32, 34, 64–65, 67–68, 115
    absolutely essential, 38
    executive, 64
    instructional, 39, 81
    pedagogical, 64
    supportive, 38
leadership and ability, 68
leadership and curriculum classes, 65
leadership and instructional effectiveness, 67
learning, sustained, 1
learning communities, 31, 38, 43, 120
learning culture, successful, 82
learning ecosystems, 9
learning environment
    collaborative, 32, 51
    consistent, 96
learning gaps, smallest, 62
Learning Journey, 73
Learning to Learn, 9
Learning Triangle, The, 102, 113
lesson and instruction, 102
lesson assessment, 26
lesson-implementation skills, 101
lesson objectives, 102, 104–106
lesson planning, 8, 22–23, 42–43, 70, 102, 104, 112, 119
lessons
    design, 108
    personalized, 20
    stable, 102
lesson study, 5
levels of achievement, 55
lifelong success, 15
Link, Tara, 3, 41, 114
Linked learning, 9
listener, active, 54
list of influences, 14
literacy coach, 4, 43, 77
longer school day/year, 9
long term impact, 22
Looping, 9
lunch, 117

M

Maker movement, 9
malpractice, 17
Mamluks, 28
Mass customized learning, 9
mastery, 8, 19, 78, 106, 119
mastery learning, 14, 101
Matsumoto, Shota, 65
McCluskey, Gena, 41, 114
McDonald's, 5, 75–76, 100
McKinsey & Company, 60, 71
McKinsey's Academy, 19
Meehan, Robert John, 6
mental safety, 53
Mentor, 30
mentor for survival, 26
mentoring, 7, 22, 25–32, 34–35, 70
    one-on-one, 27, 29–30
mentoring and teacher retention, relationship, 26
mentors, 6, 18, 25–31, 33, 38, 70
MetLife Survey, 5
Michael Huberman, 21
Microschools, 9
mindset, 15, 66
minority, high, 83
mise en place, 88
mission, explicit, 6
mission statement, 10, 73
misused term, 98
Moberly New Teacher Induction Program, 3, 41–43, 91, 115
model
    common teaching, 63
    successful training, 76
model classrooms, 32, 42, 47
Modular scheduling, 9
Moore Johnson, Susan, 39
Multiage classrooms, 9
Multi-classroom teachers, 9
Multicultural education, 9
Multidimensional assessment, 9
Multiple intelligence, 9
multiyear, 12, 84
Museum of Education Fads, 116
myth of individuality, 19
Myth of Mentors, 28

N

national attrition rate, 39
National Board Certification, 46
National Institute of Education, 62
Nature-based learning, 9
Needs-based education, 9
negative consequences, 98
new-teacher attrition rate, high, 81
New Teacher Induction, 1, 4, 12, 35, 46, 84, 109–111, 113, 120
New Teacher Project, 32
Nike, 121
North Carolina, 82
nourish, 20, 23, 105
novice teachers, 23, 26, 46, 49, 89, 111

O

objectives, instructional, 47, 76, 102–106, 111
obligation, professional, 115
Odysseus, 30
office, common, 5–6, 65
OJT. *See* on-the-job training
one-on-one mentoring programs, 30, 42, 70
on-the-job training (OJT), 75
Open classroom, 9
Opensource learning, 9
Outcomes-based education, 9

P

Paradigm shift, 9
participation, collective, 32
partners in reform, 71
Passion-based learning, 9
PBIS, 9
pedagogical ideology, 61, 66
pedagogical skills, 33, 63, 115
peer review, 19

peer-to-peer learning, 69
performance, teacher's, 50, 52–53
Performance assessment, 9
Personalized blended learning, 9
Personalized instruction, 9
Personal learning environment, 9
phases, professional career, 8
Phillips, Bridget, 37–39
Picting, 9
pilot training, 72
PISA rankings, 67, 69
PISA results, 68
planning, 6, 13, 50, 60–63, 69, 87, 96, 119
Play-based learning, 9
"Pledge of Allegiance, The," 91
Poland, 62, 67
Portfolio assessment, 9
positive effect on students, 14
positive learning environment, 26
power of procedures, 98
power of teamwork, 18
PowerPoint presentation, 94–95
Powley, Sarah, 110
Practice-focused curriculum, 9
practices, 17–18, 20, 24, 30, 33–34, 56, 61, 63, 67–68, 88, 102, 105, 111, 115, 117, 120
   bad, 30
   best, 6, 13, 62, 119
   collaborative, 27, 71
   daily, 98–99
   innovative, 19
   massed, 14, 101
   professional, 63
   shared, 69, 117
   successful, 31
principals, 21, 33, 47–48, 55–56, 65, 67, 71, 115
Principle-based education, 9
proactive approach, 97
Problem-based learning, 9
problem-solving groups, 6, 13, 56, 61, 69, 119
procedures
   basic, 96
   common, 38
   correct library, 101
   delivery, 74
   effective, 100
   getting started, 90
   important, 91, 98
   installed, 99
   invisible, 90, 110
   morning opening, 91
   organizational, 48
   schoolwide, 38
   standard operating, 73
professional development program
   lifelong, 12, 46, 49
   sustained, 51, 69
professional-development programs, effective, 1
professional learning, 67, 69–70, 117
professional training program, sustained, 4
professions, admired, 61
Proficiency-based learning, 9
programs
   quick-fix, 33, 84
   sustained, 12, 25, 76, 84
Project-based learning, 9
purpose, ultimate, 23

Q

questions
   common, 43
   first seven, 94
   probing, 31
   singular procedural, 31
   starter, 54
quizzes, frequent, 75

R

Ravitch, Diane, 116
Ray, Amit, 66
Reality therapy, 9
reason teachers flee, primary, 109
Reciprocal accountability, 9
Reciprocal teaching, 14, 101
recruiting, 12, 66, 80–82, 108
recruitment costs, 79
Reggio Emilia Approach, 9
relationship between mentoring and teacher retention, 26
Relationship-centered approach, 9
relationships, 39, 81, 117
   constructive, 21
   developing supportive professional, 81
   positive, 21
   productive one-on-one, 53
   student-teacher, 55
Renaissance science, 9
research, 1, 10, 14–15, 19, 26–29, 37–40, 47, 101–102, 104
research groups, 68
   teaching research/action, 70
research on mentoring, 27
research-oriented teaching, 68
research procedures, 115
resisting change, 28
resources
   human, 33, 52, 79, 84, 112
   limited, 83
   teachers study, 42
Restorative justice, 9
results, astounding, 51
retention, 23, 34, 52–53, 115
   improving, 81
retention rate, 13, 39, 62
Return on Investment (ROI), 77–78
Revolutionary learning, 9
Richardson, Joan, 17
Rockefeller Institute, 55
Rogers, Karen, 91, 95
ROI. See Return on Investment
room, teacher's, 117–119
rotating master teachers, 68
routines, 45, 47, 53, 90–91, 98, 100–101, 110
rubric, 26, 104, 106
rules, 47, 67, 73, 90, 93–94, 98
rules and consequences, 47, 90

S

Saborio, Gail A., 31
safety net, 26–27
sage-on-the-stage, 10
Schleicher, Andreas, 19, 67
School choice, 9
school district, 1, 5, 8, 10, 12, 20, 50, 66, 70–72, 79, 81, 84–85, 89, 109, 113, 115–116, 120
    urban, 11, 81, 85, 89
school district budgets, 79
schools, 1–13, 15–26, 28–29, 31–34, 37–42, 45, 47–48, 50–52, 55–56, 60–69, 71–72, 78–79, 81–85, 87–90, 94, 96, 98–99, 101, 104, 109–110, 112–113, 115–117, 119–120
    bad, 32–33
    effective, 4, 17–18, 51, 113
    ineffective, 18
    low-performing, 33, 68, 81
    underperforming, 81
school system, best, 63
school systems
    highest performing, 117
    top, 60
    world's, 60
self-assessment techniques, 103
self-confidence, 10
Self-directed learning, 9
Self-esteem, 9
self-fulfilling prophecy, 98
self-guided learning opportunities, 42
Self-regulated education, 9
Seroyer, Chelonnda, 97, 104
Service-based learning, 9
sessions
    after-school, 42
    collegial, 32
    in-service training, 10
Shanghai, 68–70
"Shanghai Secret, The," 24, 71
Shared decision making, 9
S.H.I.N.E., 41, 115
shortage, 7, 81, 108
shortages, total, 81
silver bullet, 116
simulation, 48
Singapore, 64, 117

Singh, Rima, 117
skills, 10, 16–17, 20, 28–31, 38, 48, 56, 71, 74–75, 79, 88, 90, 105, 115
skills development, 10, 74
Small class/school size, 9
social competence, 87
social creatures, 13
Social-emotional learning, 9
solution, commonsense, 81, 115
spaced practice, 14, 101
staff, 6, 17–18, 20, 23, 38, 52, 63, 81–83, 98, 109, 114–115, 117, 119
    supervisory, 47
staff developer, 32, 69, 117
staff development process, 31
standards, academic, 11–12, 45
Starbucks, 72–73, 76
Start of School Checklist, 89
start school day later, 9
Station Observation Checklist, 75
status
    probationary, 27
    socioeconomic, 15
status quo, 28
stay interview, 52–57
Stoebe, Stephanie, 99
strategies, 17, 26–28, 85, 102
    coping, 88
    effective, 39
Strength-based learning, 9
student achievement, 1, 5, 10, 14–15, 17, 19, 23–24, 29–30, 33, 38, 59, 68, 78, 81–84, 101, 104, 107, 112, 114–115
    improving, 10, 19–21, 30, 102
    increased, 5
student achievement gap, 81
student learning, 1, 10, 14–15, 17–18, 26–27, 29, 31, 42, 47, 64–66, 90, 98, 100–101, 104, 109, 112, 120
    improved, 9, 18, 113, 120
student learning strategies, 31
Student-led learning, 9
student motivation, 101
student or child-centered, 109
student performance, 83, 102
    strong, 32
students, 1, 3, 5, 7–8, 11–12, 14, 16–21, 23, 25, 33, 37–38, 41–42, 45–48, 51, 55–56, 59–61, 63, 65–68, 71, 77–79, 81–87, 89–94, 96–106, 108–113, 115, 120
    assigned low-performing, 83
    at-risk, 99
    disadvantaged, 67
    essential questions, 94
    first-grade, 91
    focused on the, 109
    high-achieving, 60
    interest, 103
    managing, 50
    special education, 78
    support, 102, 113
    tardy, 87
    teacher greets, 91
    values, 19
student success, 5, 33, 54–55, 71, 78, 101, 105, 108, 117
    increased, 17
student teaching experience, 14
student test scores, 50
Studio-based learning, 9
study groups, 13, 18, 22, 32, 51
success, 4, 8, 13–15, 18–20, 23–24, 35, 37–38, 46, 50, 52–53, 71, 76, 87–90, 98, 100–102, 104–106, 111, 115, 120
    continuous, 113
    early, 60, 87
    instructional, 113
success and achievement, 23
success criteria, 112
successful classrooms, characteristics, 21, 97, 110
success rate, 112
Success Trail poster, 37–38
superintendent, 3, 31, 33, 41, 46–48, 114
    assistant, 41, 114
survival, 8, 18, 26–27, 30–31, 70
survival attitude, 15
Swiss philosophy, 30
Systems thinking skills, 9

T

teacher attrition, 12, 37, 44, 65, 67, 78, 80, 83–85, 116
teacher certificate requirements, 1
Teacher clarity, 14, 101–102, 104, 106, 112
teacher effectiveness, 5, 10, 28, 104
Teacher Induction Program for Success. *See* TIPS
teacher networks, 18, 22, 32, 51
teacher quality, 5, 84
teacher quality gap, 81
teacher retention, 26, 38, 50, 52, 84
teachers
    crying, 122
    effective, 1–5, 10–14, 21, 23, 25, 29, 33, 37–39, 49, 51, 59, 64–65, 71, 78, 82, 84, 91, 96, 98, 101–102, 108, 110, 114–116, 119–120
    preservice, 14, 38
    recruiting, 80
    successful, 67, 71, 99
    supply and demand, 80, 108
    uncertified, 12, 81
    valuable, 53, 56
    weakest, 69, 117
teacher shortage, 12, 24, 41, 81, 116, 120
teacher workforce, 59
teaching culture, 69, 117
Teaching for social justice, 9
teaching profession, 23, 32, 61, 76
teach to objectives, 106
Team-based learning, 9
teams, 13, 18, 22, 29–30, 52, 65, 76, 105, 113, 118
teamwork, 15, 18–19, 45, 47, 66
technology, 7, 10, 19, 21, 33, 51, 59, 65, 84, 109, 115
Technology-based learning, 9
Terrell, Cathy, 94
test
    criterion-referenced, 103
    PISA, 67
Texas school districts, 33, 84
Thematic-integrated instruction, 9
Theme-based learning, 9
thinking skills, critical, 19
Three-dimensional teaching, 9

time
    ideal, 31, 53
    instructional, 90
TIPS (Teacher Induction Program for Success), 45, 47
Tomita, Renee, 90
Torff, Bruce, 101
Total Quality Management, 9
Toujouse, Megan, 92
TQM, 9
tragedy, greatest, 32, 77, 83
train, 1, 6, 11–14, 18, 23, 26–27, 37–38, 40, 45, 48–49, 51, 59, 61, 64, 68–69, 71–76, 79–85, 88–89, 97, 113, 115–16, 119
train and nurture, 51
Train the Trainer, 75
trust, 53, 87, 110, 119
turnover, 79, 83–84
    high, 18, 39, 84
    low, 84
turnover costs, 79, 81, 83
turnover rate, 81
    annual, 81
21st Century curriculum, 9

U

understanding
    better, 54
    clear, 32, 108–109
    shared pedagogical, 119
unintended consequences, 54
United Airlines, 5, 76
United States, 5–6, 8, 15, 19, 32, 39, 49, 59–60, 63, 65–67, 70, 74, 76, 78, 80, 83, 115–116
urban schools, successful, 81

V

vacancies, 81
vacancy, 38, 109
veteran teacher, 27, 65, 117

Virtanen, Pauli, 61
Virtual learning, 9
Visible Learning, 14
vision
    collective, 18
    common, 17, 31, 120

W

Wagner, Janis, 8
Walmart, 74
welcome sign, 87
welcoming gifts, 42
Wheatley, Margaret J., 54
White, Mike, 100
Whole language, 9
Williams, Roger, 113
win with people, 10
wisdom, 22, 30, 68
    acquired, 30
    impart, 30
    infinite, 77, 115
Wong, Harry, 35, 50, 71, 115, 123
Wong, Rosemary, 50, 123
Work-based learning, 9
World Economic Forum, 62
Wynn, Susan, 26

Y

Year-round schools, 9

Z

Zero tolerance, 9
Zombie-based learning, 9